THE
UNCOMMON MAN

McKINSEY FOUNDATION LECTURE SERIES

Sponsored by the
Graduate School of Business, Columbia University

THE
UNCOMMON MAN

The Individual in the Organization

CRAWFORD H. GREENEWALT

President, E. I. du Pont de Nemours & Company

McGraw-Hill Book *Company,* Inc.
NEW YORK TORONTO LONDON 1959

PREFACE

It is the thesis of this book that all organizations, nations, societies, and civilizations will prosper and advance only to the extent that they can encourage common men to perform uncommon deeds. Only thus will emerge The Uncommon Man. Every human association depends on the individual; on his skills and on his acceptance of responsibilities to conduct organizational affairs with effectiveness. Yet, there are those who would say that individual freedom and personal development are circumscribed by the fact of association in large organizations, including large-scale business corporations.

In the third series of McKinsey Foundation lectures held during the Spring of 1958 at the Graduate School of Business of Columbia University, Mr. Crawford H. Greenewalt, the President of E. I. du Pont de Nemours, addressed himself to this centrally significant problem. This book, based on those lectures, provides an intimate glimpse of the mind of one of America's foremost business leaders. Mr. Greenewalt takes pains *not* to hide his own thinking about the problems of the individual in his relationship to large-scale business. In his treatment of the subject he reveals incisively not only the nature of a large and successful company, but the personality of its top executive officer.

It is a measure of the personality of Crawford Greenewalt that while preparing these lectures, and their expansion into this volume, he was occupied not only with the management of a large company but with another literary venture which I am told is a definitive study of the life and habits of the hummingbird. This versatility reflects that diversity of interest characteristic of humanists through the ages. The requirements of a heavy schedule have not detracted one bit from the penetrating insights presented in this lucidly styled volume.

Much has been written in recent decades of the pressure toward conformity in large organizations. By no means does Mr. Greenewalt dispute this danger. He does distinguish, however, between debilitating conformity of thought and rational conformity of behavior within the bounds of commonly accepted purpose and good manners. Excessive conformity, it is pointed out, is a danger in organizations of all sizes, irrespective of the purposes for which they exist. It may be as prevalent in small as in large organization, in the quiet village as well as in the throbbing metropolis.

Stimulation of uncommon effort and suppression of pressures toward conformity requires a conscious and continuing effort to maximize both personal freedom and incentives. This is Mr. Greenewalt's cardinal precept of management. Its elaboration involves observations among a wide range of topics of interest to students of management: executive selection, evaluation and training, tax policies, financial compensation and other incentives, and even the shifting relationships between ownership and salaried management.

This is no simple analysis, nor should one expect all of the prescriptions to enlist total acceptance. It is a virtue of this forthright excursion into management psychology, economics and social organization that in its preparation the author has without intent demonstrated the qualities of The Uncommon Man. He has personified his own prescription.

Under the direction of Dr. Leonard R. Sayles of

the Graduate School of Business faculty, digests of the discussions which followed the lectures were made and a portion of their content has been incorporated into the text. Mr. Greenewalt has, however, amended the lectures by the addition of a considerable quantity of new and original material. In the process, he has enlarged substantially the measure of his thesis and has given a new and impressive dimension to the case for The Uncommon Man.

COURTNEY C. BROWN
Dean, Graduate School of Business
Columbia University

CONTENTS

Some men are uncommon to extraordinary degree, others to lesser. And perhaps most uncommon of all is the common man whose achievements are exalted beyond the expectation of his circumstances.

THE
UNCOMMON MAN

ATMOSPHERE FOR
ACHIEVEMENT

The United States of America was founded on the "grand scheme and design" of human freedom. Its premise was the conviction that society can profit most through emancipation of the individual from all forms of power—economic, political, or social—which impose unnatural restraints against his full development.

With equality of opportunity fully guaranteed, each man could rise to whatever heights his talents and his desires might lead. In this way, the nation declared its trust in human dignity and in human achievement, signifying a faith that man, given adequate encouragement, can find in himself unsuspected resources of performance and aspiration.

The story of America is the story of common men who, whatever their motives, whatever their goals, were inspired to uncommon levels of accomplishment. Just as many drops of water can join to

1

make a waterfall, increments of human accomplishment, small perhaps for any individual, will, when multiplied by millions, create a nation whose stature is second to none. This is America, these her uncommon men.

I do not deprecate the unusually gifted individuals to whom we must be eternally grateful for their contributions in many different areas. To Franklin, to Eli Whitney, to Lincoln, and to our long list of Americans of superior capacities, we owe a great debt. But such as these do not make a nation any more than a single beautiful flower makes a garden. I would guess that the proportion of outstanding individuals in any nation, and at any time, would prove fairly constant, and would be independent of the political climate in which they lived. After all, genes and chromosomes are not responsive to party lines, whether the atmosphere be capitalist, fascist, socialist, or the *polis* of ancient Greece. The strength of a nation is the accomplishment of its entire citizenry and it is here that the free society has had its greatest triumph.

Who can identify the qualities of mind or spirit or dedication in men which mark the division between the common and uncommon? The strengths and weaknesses of human beings cannot be catalogued as though they referred to blooded dairy stock. Some men are uncommon to extraordinary degree, some to lesser. And perhaps most uncommon of all is the common man whose achievements are exalted beyond the expectation of his circumstances.

The important thing is that we bring into play the full potential of all men, whatever their station. Whether we speak of a nation, an organization, or of our conduct as individuals, we know that people's behavior varies with conditions. Few elements in nature have the volatility of the human spirit; it is as sensitive to its environment as the flower which opens its petals in the sunlight and droops in dejection at night. The challenge is to create an atmosphere in which men, whatever their level of talent, gain through their association with one another. When this condition exists, those of lesser gifts are drawn upward by the precept and example of those whose abilities are greater. And those of higher attainments are elevated toward new peaks of achievement with the rising level of the average.

"Less than in the sum total of their abilities," observed Charles Darwin in *Origin of Species*, "men differ in the *degree to which they use them.*"

In the game of tennis which I play, I am afraid, with greater enthusiasm than aptitude, I most often find myself matched with others whose skill greatly exceeds my own. The effect is to drive me to efforts considerably beyond my normal performance. Similarly, I have observed that a really fine player loses his touch and appears quite ordinary when he is simply killing time with an indifferent adversary.

In all sports, we see people "playing over their heads," as it is said.* And so in any activity, the task is to set up the game in such a way as to produce this result.

Today, the complexities of life in the United States are such that recognition of the individual contribution becomes increasingly difficult. The great problem is the harmonizing of personal achievement with the needs of a society many times larger and more intricate than that of the early days and in which the old-fashioned values of self-reliance, thrift, and industry seem to have lost some of their appeal. How, then, can we bring forward superior qualities of accomplishment and resolution

---

* I am not much of a baseball fan, but I am impressed by one baseball legend: "When you put on the uniform of the New York Yankees," said one player, "you grow three inches!" A significant testimonial to the effects of such morale is the fact that, in ten years, the Yankees have won pennants nine times. But only two players on the 1958 team were on the scene in 1948!

when the incentives and inspiration toward singularity of performance seem to be declining?

How can we maintain the identity of the individual in a world which increasingly must turn to the group or the organization for progress?

How can we preserve our personal liberties in the face of needs and demands which appear to call for collective rather than individual effort?

I would contend that the experience of the American business organization offers as good a laboratory as we have to study the factors which influence our society. The corporation, like society itself, is a congregation of human beings and, like society itself, it prospers to the extent that the relationships it maintains are fruitful, harmonious, and mutually beneficial.

The statistics are sufficiently impressive to set at rest any question as to the general relevance of industrial effort. More than 12,000,000 people own a share of the American business and industrial community. Activity in the field of manufacture, which has long since passed agriculture as the principal occupation of the American worker, is the most critical index of national prosperity. In employment, the 500 largest U. S. industrial firms alone employ nearly 9,000,000 workers. Joined by wives

and families, this represents a total of perhaps 35,-
000,000 people, more than the combined population of the Atlantic seaboard states from Maine to
North Carolina and larger than the entire population of the United States in 1860.

The significance of any institution of such vast
dimension seems self-evident. As the principal instrument through which industry is carried on in
this country, the corporation is thoroughly characteristic of Twentieth Century America. Four out of
five breadwinners today are employed persons, in
direct contrast to the situation of a hundred years
ago when four out of five earned their livings as
independent enterprisers or as artisans, farmers, or
seasonal workers whose employment was periodic
and uncertain. A substantial number work not in
groups of a dozen or a score, but as members of
large-scale corporate organizations whose enrollments run into many thousands.

In many respects, therefore, the modern corporation is a slice of society in microcosm. Its personnel
is drawn from all levels and all elements of the
population as a whole and, as such, represents a
segment of the public itself. And as a human institution, relying wholly upon the effort of human
beings, it would seem that the factors influencing

corporate growth and progress are identical to those applicable to society as a whole. Every circumstance bearing upon the motivation and the response of the individual in one is paralleled in the other; the human relationships by which men live are common to both.

If the use of a commercial organization as a case study seems presumptuous, it is only because such references are unusual, reflecting, I am afraid, a rather patronizing attitude toward the American business community. The American businessman has not been too skillful in merchandising his professional qualifications. He has been neglected by the historian, scorned by the litterateur, and snubbed by the social critic. In the stuff of which heroes are fashioned, he is well down the list, less romantic than the pirate or the cowboy, less spectacular than the soldier, less portentous than the statesman. There is apparently nothing in the business suit quite so glamorous as epaulets or cutaway.

Modern business has no patron saint and no oath hallowed by centuries of devotion; it is, for the most part, a profession without traditions. But the day is long behind us when Henry and William James could dismiss the business area rather contemptuously as "trade." Whatever he is, the businessman is the product and the pilot of the system under which most of us earn our livings. He is the instrument through which our technological progress is transmitted to the public use and benefit. And the organization through which he operates would seem to have become a valid and significant sample of our society.

As to my own qualification as a spokesman, I must assume that this arises out of my association with the Du Pont Company and what I can say as a result of that association about the Company's business philosophies. The Du Pont Company, as a matter of fact, does occupy a unique place among American institutions and so offers an opportunity to examine the elements leading to growth and progress in a business experiment which has extended over a very long period of time. It is a large company —the largest producer of chemical products in the United States, perhaps in the world. But the singularity of this company does not lie in its size or in the industrial area in which it now operates, but in the fact that, since its beginnings in 1802, through all varieties of social and economic climate, it has grown and prospered.

Many large companies today are in a relatively early stage of development and, as institutions, they are still, as Emerson put it, the lengthened shadow of a man. Du Pont, on the other hand, has had ten presidents, and its founder has been dead well over a century, so its shadow is not that of a man, but of men, just as its history is not that of a generation or an era, but of a span of years almost equal to that which the nation has endured. A single season, a single year, a single brilliant individual will create a corporate image quite different and much less relevant to our discussion than one which is the synthesis of many seasons, many years, and a long succession of individuals.

So, to any examination of organizations in America today, Du Pont has its value as a case study, not in its personalities, but in its principles, and more particularly as a demonstration of a factor I believe to be of critical importance to any human activity.

Here is an organization which has been able, over the years, to enlist and to maintain the serious effort of a host of individuals who, if we can accept the usual criteria of success, have been above the average in effectiveness. There is no reason to believe that Du Pont, as an institution, has had access to men who differed greatly in caliber or training from those who might have associated themselves with any other institution. I think we can assume that the human raw material over the years would be assessed as average and neither better nor worse than any other group of comparable size and variety.

This being the case, it must be clear that there is something in the environment which has inspired average men to above-average performance, and it is this fact that seems most significant in its application to all organizations.

I do not think the answer is mysterious or in any way unique. It seems clear that the Du Pont Company's success over this long period has come about in large part through devoted allegiance to two major theses:

First, the realization that an enterprise will succeed only to the extent that all individuals associated with it can be encouraged to exercise their highest talents in their own particular way. Second, the provision of maximum incentives for achievement, particularly in associating the fortunes of the individual with that of the corporation.

Each of these bench marks of policy is dedicated to the purpose of preserving and implementing individual achievement, an objective which is no less vital today when Du Pont is a large company than it was in the beginning when it was a very small company. Eleuthere Irénée du Pont believed firmly, with Jefferson, that effort and achievement would exceed all expectations if the energies and imaginations of men could be freed of restrictions and restraints. Study of the environment most conducive to individual effort, therefore, appears to have particular relevance.

The Du Pont Company's top management group, including the members of the Executive Committee and the heads of the manufacturing and auxiliary departments, totals thirty-four. Considered as individuals, I am afraid the only common characteristic I can recognize in my associates is that they are all very able men and all, in their own way, rugged individualists. Beyond that, the differences between them are almost bewildering in their variety. No two of them will approach a particular problem in quite the same way, and no one of them could do his job nearly so well if he were required to do it according to some preconceived and generalized executive pattern.

We have a highly decentralized organization, and I might say parenthetically that this requires much in the way of individual forbearance. One man may well chafe, for example, at a successor's approach to a job, or a subordinate's handling of a problem. It is only human to think highly of one's own method, and it calls for Christian tolerance to reach the understanding required to endorse methods and approaches which are not one's own. But it is the result that counts, and when one looks past method to accomplishment, it is easy to see that, within a given area of principle, there are many ways in which a good job can be done—as many ways, in fact, as there are men to whom the task might be given.

The insistence that method be left to the individual is a basic premise. Sometimes, this makes it very difficult to get any advice at all. When I was elected president, there were still very much on the scene not less than four previous presidents of our Company. All had offices on the same floor as mine, and usually all four were on hand daily.

You might think that, in such a situation, I would not lack for advice or suggestions. Far from it! In my early days of uncertainty, I used to go from one to the other and ask how they would approach this problem or that. I had a terrible time getting any answers at all!

"Well, now, whatever you think," they would say. I would press on, hoping for some concrete thought, some ray of illumination. But only with the greatest reluctance would any of them offer an opinion. Not once has one of them ever come to me with a gratuitous suggestion.

To the man who follows me, I can only say, "From the day you take over, it's up to you. If you want general hints, there is much tradition and some literature. I expect to take my ease and watch you do the work."

The delegation of authority and the principle of individual laissez-faire extends throughout the organization. At each organizational level, sufficient authority is delegated to enable the individual concerned to discharge adequately the responsibilities associated with his particular post.

In authority and responsibility, however, we encounter a rather odd paradox. Authority can and must be delegated; responsibility can never be. For even though one officer may delegate to a subordinate full authority for conducting the affairs of a department or an activity, the ultimate responsibility remains his own. Our Executive Committee assigns responsibility to a department head, but the Committee itself is equally responsible to the Board of Directors for its performance; in fact, for all sins of commission and omission wherever they may occur. The situation can be likened to the old tale of the magic pitcher, in which, no matter how much water was poured out, the remaining level was always the same. No matter how much responsibility we assign to others, our own stands undiminished.

I suppose the difference between good management and bad can be said to depend upon how it deals with this question of shared responsibility. If a manager interprets his duties as requiring him to stand with his hand eternally on his subordinate's shoulder, he is a poor manager and his subordinate cannot possibly do his job well. The alternative, of course, is to give him every opportunity to do the job in his own way, with whatever general guidance is necessary. If he fails, one must admit to a bad initial choice and look for a better replacement.

These alternatives frequently leave one suspended between frying pan and fire. If a poor job is being done, there is always the temptation to step in and take over and, to some, this seems the more humane course. It takes far more courage to admit to a poor selection, but that recognition and the unpleasant replacement process is far better for the business, and, in the long run, kinder to the misplaced incumbent. Forbearance is indeed an essential management attribute, but it is useless if the courage is lacking to be tough-minded in recognizing and facing up to the deficiencies of the man who fails to click.

The problem of filling responsible positions with competent candidates is one of the most important management functions. In our Company, some thirty management positions in the levels above plant manager must be filled each year. When all supervisory levels are considered, someone has calculated that there is a promotion somewhere in the Du Pont Company every ten working minutes. Obviously, intelligent selection is a critical matter. We believe in frequent and thorough appraisals and, if there is anything which characterizes our approach, it is to expose people to a variety of judgments by shifting their locale both functionally and departmentally.

In each of these phases of operation and practice, there is the inherent principle of dealing with people as individuals. This is comparatively simple to achieve in a small, closely knit organization although, even there, many of the factors of modern life suggest the general rather than the particular, the mass rather than the man. In a large organization where these factors operate with multiplied effect, it is a difficult job indeed. It requires constant application.

Nevertheless, the effort goes on, compromised perhaps to the extent necessary by changing conditions, but always firmly in mind. We try to encourage our supervision to regard those under their charge as associates; as human beings with aspirations and goals as diverse as their physical features. Only if these personal circumstances are recognized and respected can the identity of the individual be preserved. Only in this way can the individual make his most significant contribution.

Some of the critics of modern society apparently see the human race today as becoming more and more like a housing development with each member as the serial expression of a master plan. I am not convinced that the conclusion is wholly valid, and I am not at all sure that the concept can be termed modern in any respect. Original thinking has never found a ready-made acceptance, as men have learned through many generations.

Back in 1902, a very wise administrator in the Du Pont Company wrote into our first incentive plan a provision which perhaps anticipated this trait of human nature. It is part of that plan today. It provides that, in setting awards, special consideration be given to individuals who achieved a goal "in the face of objection, from within or without."

It has always seemed to me that this provision characterizes the spirit of individual effort. Perhaps "conformity" represented a clear danger as far back as that day when the architects of the plan with their swirling mustaches, stiff collars, and high-button shoes saw the need of goading the timid and diffident and offered special rewards to those who would break through the barriers. The offer is still open and, as long as its spirit is maintained, we face the future with high confidence.

THE NATURE
OF ORGANIZATIONS

I am always a little suspicious of categorical pronouncements about change. In every era, there are those who proclaim that everything is entirely different from what it used to be, for better or for worse, depending on the disposition of the proclaimer. Searching analysis, however, often shows that only the superficialities are different and that the fundamentals of human behavior have changed very little. Perhaps this is why the French, an old and wise people, often observe "the more things change, the more they are the same."

The changes which have come about in the Twentieth Century are, of course, obvious and startling in their physical expression, although some of the social phenomena which worry us now are not wholly without precedent. Reviewing some dusty old newspaper files not long ago, I was not too surprised, for example, to note that, in 1902, the year I was born, editorialists were worrying themselves about automobile accidents, divorces, and labor disputes, problems which have stubbornly resisted both technological and spiritual progress.

Nonetheless, in the area of industrial enterprise, the changes in scale alone are sufficient to justify the conviction that something really new has appeared. Manufactures we have always had, but now we see a technology under which a small-town steam laundry becomes vastly more complex than the largest industrial establishments of an earlier day. Corporations date from medieval times, yet now we experience corporate activity of a dimension which would have bewildered heads of state a century ago.

Individualism was still very much the order of the day in the early 1900's. Business houses were identified with their principal officers or proprietors. Newspapers were the personal voices of their editors and publishers. Colleges were linked with the names of their presidents—Harvard was Dr. Eliot, for example, just as Princeton was Dr. Wilson, and Columbia was Nicholas Murray Butler.

Mention of Standard Oil meant John D. Rockefeller, in person; the Morgan Bank was J. P. Morgan himself, just as the *Louisville Courier* was

Henry Watterson and the *New York World* was Joseph Pulitzer. The labor movement was Samuel Gompers. And the electric light belonged to Thomas Edison, the telephone to Alexander Graham Bell, and the Ford car to Henry Ford himself.

Today, the emphasis has passed from these colorful and personable individuals to somewhat austere and anonymous institutions. We recognize corporate anonymity in our titles, General Electric and General Motors, for example, and U. S. Steel and Standard Oil. Perhaps these impersonal designations are no more than tacit recognitions of the fact that no single individual, no matter how gifted, can any longer embrace the increasing complexity of our technology and the innumerable facets of modern corporate effort. Our major enterprises have developed into entities owned, not by their proprietors or founders, but by thousands of stockholders, and managed, not by one man, but by many, and the relative importance of any individual at any given time is quite properly less a matter for public concern than the soundness and the continuity of the institution.

This phenomenon is by no means limited to the sphere of business. We have large labor unions, large government, large educational institutions, in all of which the complexities of today's problems have outgrown the capacity of the single gifted personality. Even in science, long the domain of the lone worker, we can now rarely attribute an invention to a single individual. Radar and television are household terms, but we would be hard pressed to name a single scientist importantly associated with their development.

What has been happening for a great many years has been the gradual and inevitable merger of individual effort into group effort. Group effort has always been with us, of course. Man is a social animal, as Aristotle noted, and a latter-day philosopher was to add that "an entirely isolated man would perish as an undiscriminated object in the chaos of nature."

Teams of laborers built the pyramids and teams of craftsmen the medieval cathedrals. Now, for the first time, however, management itself has become a team effort with group direction, group initiative, and group responsibility. This comes about quite naturally. As our economy grows in size and stature, only the smallest of institutions, commercial or otherwise, can be encompassed and directed by a single head. As our technical virtuosity increases, we have greatly enlarged our demands for men with specialized skills to follow trails which the uncommitted pioneer finds too diffuse to pursue alone.

Whether we applaud or condemn these social patterns, the transition continues, and it is to the organization rather than the individual that we look as the responsible instrument of human achievement. Men and women congregate in groups and organizations to meet complexities and challenges too sweeping for personal solutions. We are coming to regard the constellation rather than the star, the forest rather than the tree, the sea rather than the wave. To meet these needs, we have created institutions equal in size and scope to their responsibilities. Some of them are very large indeed, not only in production and commerce where we have heard so much of the Goliath, but actually in all fields. There were, in 1902, few colleges—perhaps none—with enrollments of more than 5,000; today, there are a great many. In 1902, the student bodies of the 10 largest together would scarcely fill today's freshman form at New York University or the University of California.

Government itself has become an enormous complex employing one in ten of our working population. Any one of the national labor groups now embraces more members than the entire working population not too many generations ago. Even our churches have had to organize to fulfill their enlarged responsibilities.

The growth in scale and relative importance of the corporation is a familiar story. The chances are remote that there is anyone who, in one capacity or another, can go very long without contact with one of our large-scale enterprises. Indeed, the national conviction seems to be that progress in any field requires the creation of an organization. There are now, it is estimated, more than 200,000 leagues, committees for or against, lodges, councils and clubs in the country dedicated in one way or another to improving things, even some things which, so far as I can see, need no improving whatever.

At any rate, we have reared a formidable structure indeed in the modern organization, and our great problem is to learn how best to live with it, inside and out.

Learning our lesson in this respect requires, first, that we understand the fundamental nature of the organization itself. With an increasing population and a desire for improved material benefits, men seemed to understand early that some form of organization would be required and some adjustments and reconciliations would become necessary.

As the scale increased, however, they came to view the Twentieth Century creation with a curious mixture of admiration and fear. We boast about the size of our institutions and their capabilities; we delight in the creation of an industrial Paul Bunyan in modern dress. At the same time, we fear the result; we distrust the power we conceive the organization may wield in our normal lives.

This misunderstanding appears to arise from an image of the organizational structure not as a body of people joined together for common good, but as some sort of monster or automaton with a life and will of its own. Woodrow Wilson, writing before World War I, misinterpreted the issue along with many of his contemporaries. After describing quite appropriately some of the difficulties facing the individual in the corporation, Mr. Wilson concluded that the way to salvation was simply to assume that the organizations into which men had joined themselves were of themselves evil and must be "humanized through direct action of law."

In this kind of misconception, we have perhaps the origin of the curious demonology which, even today, leads to the conclusion that a challenge to individual identity is an inherent characteristic of the corporate structure. Recently, Mr. Adolf Berle, under the auspices of the Fund for the Republic, has been discussing the corporation in terms of its supposed "power," a distrustful concept which shows through despite his careful, moderate tone.

Mr. Berle believes that protection of the individual must come through some kind of doctrine subjecting corporations to the same rules as affect agencies of the government. Under one rule, he says that corporations should be required to observe the Bill of Rights. I had until then been unaware that corporations had any such exemptions. Corporate "powers" are a myth as far removed from reality as Aladdin's lamp or Jack's extraordinary beanstalk.

Any corporation, it seems to me, has its own system of checks and balances and is probably more sensitively responsive to public will than is government itself. The reason is that the business organization, in addition to its internal controls, is subject to the sovereignty of the market place, a force which can express itself more rapidly and with greater effect than a thoroughly aroused and indignant electorate. I know of no corporate therapy which can immunize against customer sanctions. Certainly size is of small avail in dealing with the angry lady at the store counter once she has her dander up and her umbrella swinging.

Organizations, corporate or otherwise, are not inanimate objects, composed of steel or brick or equipment, but living mechanisms made up of human beings. In whatever field a given organization operates, it is nothing more than the sum total of the talents, the aspirations, and the characters of the human building blocks of which it is made, mellowed perhaps by the traditions and collective experience left behind by other human beings who have gone before. To speak of "humanizing" by force of law would seem to me to place a low premium indeed upon the integrity and sincerity of the human race itself.

The essential characteristics of an organization do not change with growth. What was a small body of men and women becomes a larger group. And whether it is large or small, or whether commercial, spiritual, or cultural in purpose, it represents a segment of humanity. As institutions, all organizations recruit their people from the same melting pot, the same source which supplies the human raw material for all other trades or vocations. Thus, they represent a cross-section of society—the brilliant and the dull, the generous and the grasping, the expansive and the petty, the good and the bad. Grouped together, the weakness in one is compensated by strength in another, the exuberance of the young is tempered with the steadiness and wisdom of the mature.

Hence, the organization is nothing more than a slice of life. Whatever individual dispositions may be present, it is the average, the composite which must prevail. Decisions made in the name of the organization are still human decisions, and, as organizations, we are still subject only to the human will. If we can concede that people in the main have decent and honorable instincts, it must necessarily follow that, when they join together, the character of the organization will average out at about the same moral level.

In any organization, too, there will be an added pressure for conformity to the public interest arising simply out of the sheer numbers of people involved in any given decision—the larger the organization, the larger this number becomes. Thus, organizational conduct will in itself reflect the public interest as it may exist in a particular setting and at a particular time.

A disposition on the part of a single individual within the organization to be a scoundrel would encounter tough going. The number of people he would have to persuade to join him on the primrose path would, I think, dishearten the most determined. Anyone seriously committed to a life of crime could certainly find far more fruitful opportunities than exist in the field of business management.

No, the danger does not lie with any inherent evil on the part of the organization, but in quite another direction—one to which no law nor legislation can apply. The hazard is that the very pressures within the group which hold the scoundrel in check will impose upon the individual restrictions which stifle the creative urge and the zeal for personal achievement.

If I were faced with a choice between a society which sublimated the good with the bad, I think I would rather take my chances with the scoundrels than risk losing the creative force unleashed by a free rein on individual effort. I am sure the country's long-term interest would sustain me here. To play Mark Antony in reverse, it seems to me that the evil which men do survives them only a short time, whereas the good, far from being interred with their bones, goes on and on forever. And the good which all men accomplish can be no more than the sum of their individual accomplishments.

INCENTIVES
AND
REWARDS

All of us, I suppose, have at one time or another been exposed either as child or as parent to that ancient scholastic complaint which goes, "It isn't that he's stupid, he just doesn't try." Or, "Johnny isn't doing as well as he *could* do."

The school room is perhaps our first encounter with the problems of motivation and incentive and, as such, is a testing ground, not only for the student, but for the teacher as well. If Johnny fails to apply himself, he is properly chided and made to do his homework. The teacher, in the long run, will be judged on his ability to inspire high performance in his classroom.

It seems to me that this commonplace childhood experience can be projected directly to the larger institutions encountered in our adult lives, to corporations, to organizations of all kinds; indeed, to the public welfare generally. For none of us changes very much in our responses or reactions as we grow older. Given the right stimulus, we tackle our jobs eagerly and perform them well. With indifferent leadership or discouraging surroundings, we tend to coast and our minds and ambitions atrophy. Boy or man, our performance responds to external influences through which effort can be either magnified or vitiated.

The unique aspect of American achievement is the fact that our people have enjoyed, from earliest times, the heady heritage of freedom, the strongest and most dynamic economic force the world has yet seen. For centuries, the world had put its trust in the rather cynical notion that men worked only out of urgent necessity and could be kept busy only if they were kept poor. Our new idea was that inducements and incentives for accomplishment would be of much greater effectiveness under the proposition that reward, or hope of reward, would unleash energies and talents to a degree hitherto unknown.

This has remained a basic precept of our society. The scale of values undergoes continual reshaping and may differ widely with individuals and with areas of activity, but the principle remains. Nations and institutions prosper and advance in proportion to their success in stimulating the most effective effort of each individual.

The United States stands today as the summation of such individual endeavors. It is the synthesis of the efforts of many millions, past and present, striving for goals which, while differing widely, seemed to those concerned to be worth their while. To each has been given the opportunity, at whatever the level of his abilities, to do his best.

The responsibility of management in any organization is to provide such conditions as will inspire, among as large a group as possible, the unusual rather than the perfunctory effort. I suppose it may be said that, in an ideal state of grace, men would be impelled to give of their best by simple altruism and be indifferent to the climate in which they labor and the rewards offered for success. Perhaps they should. Perhaps indeed there are many such individuals; I am inclined to think there is more idealism in the world than is usually believed. Pure altruism, however, has seldom proved the ultimate answer to human problems. (Cicero, in the First Century B. C., was moved to note rather tartly that "philosophers inscribe their names on the very books in which they urge us to despise all glory.")

Human nature being what it is, I doubt that enough of us would prove sufficiently selfless to respond without some personal lures. For most people, maximum effort is allied closely to inducements which they can identify as promoting personal interest.

Here, I realize, I risk an indignant rejoinder, for everyone likes to think he is doing his best and that he needs no special persuasion to make him do so. Yet, satisfaction with one's own performance, while providing some measure of comfort to the participant, does little to reassure management as to the future of the organization. Satisfaction is largely a subjective matter resulting from self-appraisal, and I am not sure that many of us are sufficiently strict judges of our own performance. That inner glow associated with a job well done can all too easily become a resting place for ambition and a safe backwater in which to relax. The question is not whether we are doing an adequate job, or even a good job, but whether or not we are using to maximum effect the abilities with which we are endowed. Management, with the prime responsibility of filling its own shoes, needs above anything else numbers of men willing to explore the full limit of their capabilities. It must provide whatever inducements are necessary to encourage them to do so. The question is what kinds of inducement.

√ Not all people will respond to the same stimuli. Some are powered by compulsive or obsessive drives which are sufficient unto themselves and eliminate all need for external influence. We have all observed the individual who seems unable to endure a subordinate role; no matter how casual the game, he plays to win. Others may be sufficiently inspired by the well-being of the organization with which they are associated, still others by the fulfillment of a self-imposed responsibility.

Can management, however, rely upon these internal motivations to supply an adequate number of outstanding individuals for the replacement process? I think not. Prudent operation, it seems to me, requires that such matters not be left to chance.

External motivations or incentives may take a variety of forms. Perhaps one of the more obvious is the incentive implicit in courtship. Man in pursuit of maid portrays quite graphically the Toynbee thesis of challenge and response. Under the lure of the lady's charms, the swain is assiduous in his attentions—the shoes are polished, the trousers pressed, the face razored twice daily. No task is too great. No opportunity is overlooked to express, by floral or poetic tribute, the substance of his suit.

Such tactics, while subject to rather lamentable reversals once the quarry has been brought to net, are aggressive and unremitting while the "incentive" exists. Without it, the ardor of the campaign cools and our young man is himself again—which is to say, content to rest upon his laurels.

All fields of endeavor, even those of a most selfless and spiritual nature, offer inducements and rewards to those who make a special contribution. In the academic world, professional and personal prestige have a certain magnetism which is more valued than financial remuneration. Politics afford an opportunity for public notice which, to some, is highly attractive. The arts and the theater have the goal of fame, applause, and the limelight. In pure science, there is the distinction which goes with its highest awards such as the Nobel Prize. In the armed services, incentive is based on rank and perquisites; even the churches have their hierarchies and symbolic tokens of advancement.

Older cultures than our own set great store by titles and associations of special distinction. A British subject may aspire to be a C. B. E., Sir John or even Lord So-and-So. A prewar German could hope to be "Graf," a Frenchman "M. le Compte," or an Italian "Commendatore." The Soviet Union, that haven of anonymous service, has been obliged after bitter experience to recognize the fact that people are human after all and may be expected to react best to human stimuli. It is reported that the Soviet has established incentives and emoluments which wink at the whole concept of socialized economics. For scientific accomplishment, the hook is baited with a long series of prizes including cash in amounts of many thousands of rubles which, I am told, the winners accept with quite unsocialistic eagerness and aplomb. In addition, distinction brings a range of showy medals and resounding titles such as "Hero of the Soviet Union," entitling the bearer to certain perquisites and exemptions. Some rather unusual benefits have also been devised, one being listed as preferred seats at the opera. I am uncertain as to the general applicability of opera as an attraction, but presumably the Soviets think well of it, and their recent successes cannot be shrugged aside.

I have no thought of debating either the attractions or the propriety represented by the inducements offered in different areas. Up to a point, we take some of them more or less for granted. The important thing is that they be sufficient, in each field, to bring forth the best effort on the part of those who elect to pursue them, whatever their purpose.

It seems clear that whatever the field of activity the flame of extraordinary effort shines brightest when extraordinary fuel is employed in its behalf. In the business area, as indeed in others, we hear a great deal today about environmental factors as inducements and these are, of course, important to the issue. A favorable environment in an organization reflects a leadership which one trusts and respects, an absence of restraints limiting individual development, assurance to the individual of recognition, opportunity, fair treatment. We start with the assumption that the employee who finds himself uncertain on these grounds will look elsewhere for opportunity and appropriate reward.

A favorable environment in business, in fact, is not very different from the good manners which are so important to our private associations. A true concern for the rights and privileges of people is as essential to a healthy organizational climate as it is to pleasant social intercourse among individuals and it requires of management a sincerity transcending the superficial joviality which sometimes passes for cordial human relations.

In providing incentives in an organization, I suppose the program might embrace a series of tailor-made attractions giving recognition to the particular individual's needs. Some years ago, we canvassed a small sample of our people on what non-financial job dividends would be most rewarding to them. The responses varied so widely that it was difficult to form any pattern. People differ as much in their needs and their situations as they do in their physical dimensions, and generalities concerning them are as unserviceable as shirts made in one standard size. The opportunity to travel, for example, may appeal to the man with no home ties, but will be utterly lost on the father of four small children.

The light literature of the day, backed fervently by Hollywood, seems to make quite a point of the luxury of office appointments as a source of executive satisfaction. This may or may not be true, but, in either event, it is not a question which can be answered categorically. I recall that one of our vice presidents had a wall built to cut down the proportions of his office which resembled, when he got through, a monastic cell. Another was, at the same time, enlarging his quarters and installing a desk the size of a small flight deck. Both, I wish to emphasize, were very able men.

Of all the motivations to which the human mechanism responds, however, none has proved so powerful as that of financial gain. Although the Midas complex has long since become a rarity, self-enrichment is a dream which must rank with the most compelling forces in shaping the destinies of the human race. It has always been so, and when we are disturbed over being members of a "materialistic generation," we can look back over history and note that we are simply expressing a basic human trait. With Petrarch, we may gaze at the ships hazardously bound out from Venice for remote outposts of empire and muse, "So far does love of gain stimulate the human mind."

The importance of a financial lure is not that the accumulation of wealth is in itself significant, but because money is the only form of incentive which is wholly negotiable, appealing to the widest possible range of seekers. As people differ so markedly, it is difficult if not impossible to apply any other common denominator of inducement fully acceptable to all. Money was invented for the precise purpose of providing a means of meeting widely dissimilar desires—just as meaningful to the man who wants to travel as to the father of four who is thinking about his educational responsibilities.

Despite its virtues as a medium of exchange and its ancient and universal attractions, the popular

attitude towards wealth and its acquisition has always been marked by a curious ambivalence. From
St. Paul's time to the present, "moneygrubbing"
has been denounced periodically as a social evil.
Public mention of wealth is classified by the moral
arbiter as a monstrous indelicacy and, while seeking
money is permissible up to a point, admissions ac-
knowledging such objectives are derided as vulgar.

Scholars of early times, maintaining an air of
studied indifference to fiscal matters but nonetheless dependent upon a supply of cash for bodily
comforts, had sewn into the folds of their academic
hoods a small pouch. The admiring townsfolk could
express their admiration by tossing coins into the
wide opening at the hood's back from which they
would trickle down into the pouch. Thus the
learned man could receive his stipend and appraise
it in privacy without suffering the indignity of the
extended palm. In an academic procession in which
I participated not long ago, I discovered that the
pouch, though ignored, I regret to say, by onlookers
is still a part of the doctoral hood.

So much has been made of the "vulgarity" theme
that many people—particularly many young people
—seem to accept the premise that financial gain is
somehow less noble or less exalted in purpose than

39

other forms of reward. The effect of this rather reproachful attitude is unfortunate. Many able and useful people, while engaging in the pursuit of success as measured by financial gain, feel a sense of subconscious guilt about it and, underneath it all, are faintly apologetic as to their choice.

It has always seemed to me that shamefaced attitudes about money are uncalled for. I see nothing unworthy in the financial motive, nor do I see anything vulgar in its free exercise. I doubt, in fact, that anyone has ever devised a cleaner or more honest basis for rewarding high performance.

Is a thirst for power more acceptable? I think not; history's darkest pages seem to be those devoted to power seekers and I cannot find the ordering of other people's lives an admirable goal. Nor can I believe that there is much to be said for efforts to win the cheers of the crowd, or for mere social preening. Titles and academic honors, while gratifying to the recipient, have little value beyond the immediate person. Only vicariously may the families of the knighted Briton or the beribboned warrior share his distinctions; the reflected glow may be warm, but it cannot shine far afield.

Financial gain is, in fact, the only form of incentive fully subject to sharing with others. As such, it seems to me that it is probably the least selfish inducement of all. Whatever the scale of income, the material rewards which come the way of the individual are shared with those around him; as an incentive, they often are important only to the extent that they *can* be shared.

At lower incomes, for example, there is a sharing in the form of family comforts and conveniences, an education for the children, a small luxury for a loved one. At the upper level, the circle widens to include, through gifts and benefactions, entire communities. Our universities, our libraries, our art galleries, our churches are testimonials to the sharing process.

Money is not, in other words, a static and lifeless accumulation hoarded in miserly fashion by those who treasure it for its own sake; such legends persist largely as a remnant of the Midas story and seldom exist in fact. Like water seeking its own level, fortunes in one way or another find their way back to the general benefit.

This is not to say that money cannot and is not expended foolishly, or that its pursuit has not sometimes been accompanied by actions venal and detrimental to society. But human capacity for foolishness can by no means be confined to the fiscal area, while both venality and anti-social behavior can stem from many causes. Institutions, like vineyards, should be judged by the quality of their vintages, not by the follies of the few who misuse them.

Nor is the benefit to society accruing from the pursuit of gain any the less because, as some moralists seem to worry, social gain was not the primary intent. Adam Smith pointed out quite rightly that the individual normally enters business enterprise "intending only his own gain . . . seeking his own advantage and not that of society . . . neither intending to promote the public interest nor knowing how much he is promoting it. . . ." But, Smith concludes with equal correctness, "the study of his own advantage naturally, or rather necessarily, leads him to prefer that employment which is most advantageous to the society."

I cannot see why society should be concerned over the "intent" of its benefactors, for, if its advances were limited only to those contributions which state a high moral purpose, I am afraid it would not have gotten very far. The result is independent of the intent of those who, by the very increment of their influence, advanced the cause of others, in small degree or great. Henry Ford, through his vision and his determination, brought blessings to millions of people. Had he been content to remain a bicycle mechanic, his circle would have been small. His motive is irrelevant and of little consequence to his beneficiaries. Their only concern with his effort is that he elected to try.

Nor does it matter greatly how rewards, once acquired, are used. One man may have in mind the highest purposes—to endow a hospital, or a university, or to bequeath to society a library or an art gallery or some notable park or garden, as so many have already done. Others may have in mind a frivolous, or even a wholly selfish, purpose. Why they want it is of little importance. What is important is that they be inspired to efforts beyond those they would essay if the rainbow's end had been less alluring.

Man labors most diligently when his goals, tangible or otherwise, make his efforts seem worth while. Fifty years ago, William James wrote an essay which he called "The Moral Equivalent of War." The pressures of war, he noted, invariably bring out abilities in individuals of which neither they nor their closest associates are aware. He pointed out that war induces high personal courage, hardihood, and endeavor which might have lain dormant throughout an entire lifetime spent in a peaceful society. Through teamwork arising out of national necessity, war brings into being accomplishments in the field of science and technology, for example, which might otherwise have not been realized for many years, if at all. Mr. James was an ardent pacifist, and, while deploring the futility and destructiveness of armed conflict, he realized its extraordinary effectiveness as an incentive to high individual performance. While anxious to eliminate the cause, he admitted that, without a motivation of equal strength, men and their societies would stagnate and "human life with no use for hardihood would be contemptible."

This was his basis for seeking a "moral equivalent of war"—a set of incentives sufficiently powerful to stimulate people to the equivalent of wartime effort in a peaceful world.

I doubt that any thoughtful person can deny the validity of Mr. James' premise. Military conflicts throughout recorded history have given abundant examples of high courage, great daring, and superhuman accomplishment, and this by individuals from whom such performance could not reasonably have been expected.

War is indeed a completely futile, destructive,

and immoral exercise, but I think we must agree with James that it has produced, perhaps as a completely unintentional by-product, advances in material human progress which might not otherwise have been realized.

I make these points only to show that there are indeed hidden resources in every individual and that society progresses the more rapidly the more these resources are brought into effective operation. I am convinced that men need external as well as internal motivations and that society cannot risk the consequences of not providing them. If society could find a moral equivalent of war to the end that the same high accomplishment could be generated in a peaceful world, we would have made a miraculous discovery. The question is: What should it be?

The solution suggested by Mr. James is, I am afraid, much less convincing than his exposition of the problem. He associated the motivations of war entirely with discipline, apparently seeing some benefit *per se* in hardship and suffering. I can find no merit in this thought, and I think it is now clear that the whip of the galley master was a highly inefficient tool.

Perhaps there can never be a direct equivalent

between war and peace. Perhaps people could not maintain their spirit permanently either under pressure of war or pressure of fear. I suspect, in fact, that war is by its very nature a temporary phenomenon simply because humanity cannot for very long withstand its emotional demands.

Absent the forced-draft excitement of military effort, I am inclined to rest my case with the free society.

Freedom, though the antithesis of the coercions of military emergency, is still the most effective force for real achievement yet devised by the human mind, freedom, of course, carrying with it the existence of constructive incentives. Perhaps, over a long period of years, the inducements to high performance offered by the free society at peace will not be as dramatic as those of war. On the other hand, no one can question their morality. And there can be no question that affirmative motivations, rather than those based on fear, insecurity, panic, or force, are the most effective over the long period.

FREEDOM, INDIVIDUALITY, AND CONFORMITY

Robinson Crusoe, patrolling his solitary domain, had few worries, I take it, about infringements upon his personal liberty and his personal prerogatives. His own decisions, tastes, and preferences prevailed. When Man Friday showed up, Crusoe found it necessary, according to Defoe's account, to accommodate himself to changes of routine "occasioned by the existence of a second individual."

Thus, life on a lonely island merely underlines the fact that complete freedom, which is to say a complete absence of restraints and abridgements upon private determinations, is available only to hermits.*

---

* The social rule applied equally well to political invasions. Henry Thoreau, idly skipping stones across Walden Pond, could go Jefferson one better and conclude: "That government governs best which governs not at all."

Few of us live on desert islands, and few find the role of recluse attractive. So, to the extent that we join together with others in any form of association we must surrender some part of our independence as the price of admission, as it were, to harmonious human relationships.

Even in the most basic social unit, the family, each member suffers some dilution of personal privilege in the interest of the greater convenience and happiness of the group. We accept these limitations with such grace as is consistent with our good nature. We suffer our minor irritations, hoping that our parents and our brothers and sisters and, later on, that our wives and particularly our children will bear understandingly with those they find in us. We agree to a pattern of behavior, of daily routine and of recreation which is compatible with tastes and needs of the family group.

Family ties have, in most cases, the added strengths of devotion and understanding which render sacrifice a privilege. When the association is less personal, freedom of action is even more restricted, particularly when people are thrown together in close and perhaps involuntary proximity. The crew for the submarine *Nautilus*, for example, was chosen with extreme care and trained painstakingly, having before it the prospect of close quarters and long periods of little outside contact. In any social relationship, we are obliged not by compulsion, but by the amenities to waive certain of our rights and some of the more individualistic traits of our personalities out of deference to the general good.

How much of our personal liberty we must give up, and in what directions, is a matter determined largely by common consent. The resultant becomes the morals and manners of the period and even these are not constant but differ widely from one period to another. The licentiousness of the Restoration, for example, would have outraged the mores of the Victorian era. We take a mildly superior view of the customs of the Nineties and are mildly shocked at the flaming Twenties. Whether future generations will think of the mid-Twentieth Century with approval or censure will depend on their own viewpoint, not ours.

Despite our differences of personality, tastes and interests, most of us manage to reach the common understanding which is the basis of good manners. Good manners are, as Emerson noted, "the happy way of doing things." We accept them out of our desire to live in our social environment with the least possible friction.

As we accept those restraints, we approach, I

suppose, the condition which is so widely discussed today as "conformity." It is a loose and flabby term, like many which describe abstractions. It is evident that there is confusion between the voluntary conformity of behavior which we call good manners and the enforced conformity of thought which represents an invasion of personal rights and a brake upon our capacity to follow our own destinies.

In the social area, we bow to conventional standards without loss of self-esteem. In the realm of thought and of ideas, however, we rightfully resist any effort to submerge our personal characteristics into a dull and lifeless composite.

The question is, after all, not qualitative, but quantitative: How much, or, better, how little conformity should be tolerated? Jefferson's dictum on the forbearance of ideal government could well be transplanted to this area of human relations. Let us conform as little as is necessary to good manners, pleasant relationships, and the highest use of individual talent.

Conformity in behavior is a human necessity; conformity in patterns of thought a human danger.*

* The Communist "party line" is a fair example of a monolithic unanimity of opinion, even though members

Unfortunately, people have come in modern times to mistake one for the other. There is a strong body of opinion which assumes that the conformist is the boy who gets ahead. School boys are now given grades on their "ability to cooperate," presumably on the theory that this will advance their fortunes once they launch their careers. "Cooperation" is, of course, a necessity at any time, but the premium is and always must be on original approaches.

To the extent that it can be said to exist, conformity is not, of course, a characteristic peculiar to business, nor is it uniquely the province of the large group. It may be found in some degree in all organizations of whatever nature or size. I am inclined to think that, man for man, the large business unit represents greater opportunities for individuality and requires less in the way of conformity than other institutions—in the government service, say, or in the academic world, or in the military.

I would judge, too, that "conformity" is at least as likely, perhaps more likely, to be present in small groups as large. Adjustment to a given behavior pattern is, after all, just as obligatory in a group of ten as in a group of a thousand, with the important

could presumably dress as they pleased, grow whiskers or cultivate bizarre habits.

difference that deviations attract far more attention. It is proverbial that small towns will discipline a dissenter far more drastically than the big city would take the trouble to do. By the same token I venture that conformity is more likely to be found in a small, closely held firm with a dozen employees than in the giant corporation, if only because the range of tolerance in a group of 100,000 people must necessarily be wider than in one numbering ten or twelve.

Nevertheless, it seems to be the large business unit which attracts notice in this regard and the belief seems widely prevalent that there is a pattern to which the manners, dress, and political views of each candidate for advancement must conform. The general impression has some rather bizarre twists; someone once asked me seriously if it were not true that the Buick had been selected as the official hierarchical automobile because its many grades of size and elegance could be assigned in accordance with rank! Some popular magazines have been airing the curious conviction that the wives of business executives are screened critically as part of the criteria for promotion. A number of novels, movies, and TV shows have sounded the same theme.

I cannot speak for corporations generally, nor for any, specifically, save our own. As for our Company, I will say that such notions are sheer nonsense and I will venture as a guess that the same can be said for most. The superficial symbols like the Gray Flannel Suit—I don't own one, by the way—actually mean little. Among my most valued associates, taste in dress covers a pretty broad pattern. The same goes for personal habits, enthusiasms, and, I may say, for automobiles. I could not list offhand the kinds of cars my principal associates drive. One, I know, drives an Opel, as he never fails to proclaim its virtues; another passes me occasionally in a topless Corvette in which he wears a baseball cap. Perhaps one even has a Buick, grade and model unknown.

As for wives, I can report that, among my closest co-workers, there are, of course, a number whose ladies I have known well for many years. We live in a small town and I remember some when they were on roller skates. There are a number whose wives I know well enough to exchange a "How do you do, Mrs. Smith," "How do you do, Mr. Greenewalt," and there are a number whose marital partners, I regret to say, I have never met at all.

Emphasis on the irrelevant factors of habit and

custom and on the various fictional characteristics obscure the truth, and the truth offers sufficient challenge without inconsequential distractions. The alert and well-managed organization will be fully aware of the dangers associated with individual submersion. Progress will be made in direct proportion to the intellectual freedom of action given all the men on the team. There is nothing inherent in large organizations which closes the door to high individual performance, but the larger the organization, the more assiduously it must work at the job of keeping its channels of encouragement and recognition open and flowing.

Men as well as children can lose their way in crowds. Men in organizations can be obscured, frustrated, or overlooked; injustices may be done, indignities suffered, promise suddenly turned to indifference. It is the better part of leadership to see that it doesn't happen, that no individual is hidden behind his neighbor and his potential dissipated.

Organizations are in trouble when success causes them to be so enraptured with their accomplishments that they are moved, like Narcissus, to fashion everything in their own image. I would venture the assumption that each of us, whatever our vocation, has at some time passed through an unhappy period caused by the boss' insisting that we "do it his way" instead of letting us use the methods which fall most easily to our hand.

Great emphasis is placed on training today, particularly in that nebulous area called executive development, but too much codification in training procedures often results in perpetuating facsimiles and freezing rigid patterns of thought. Thorough training is obviously a necessity, but it must always be remembered that organizations do not make men —men make organizations. It is what they bring with them in the way of character and adaptability and fresh ideas that enrich the organizational bloodstream and insure corporate longevity.

Not only the organization, but society itself suffers when people are allowed to sacrifice identity in the damp laundry of mediocrity. Competent leadership will minimize these hazards, although, people being people, perfection in this area comes hard. There are, unfortunately, few valid standards of direct comparison among human beings, and the functions and opportunities of individuals working within an organization will obviously differ with their capacities and special competence. Contributions to the joint effort will vary in kind as they vary in importance. Creative imagination will be expressed in varying ways and in varying proportion. Some contribute in brilliant flashes of form; others through their steadiness, persistence, or the gruelling and often overlooked grind of hard routine work. The important thing to the organization is that each individual be given the opportunity to exploit his talents to the fullest and in the way best suited to his personality.

Only in this way will the organization sift its more able people to the top, and although much can be said for the high general average, it is with men of first rank that the organization as well as society itself must selfishly be most concerned. The role of the common man has been widened and improved, and it operates in a great variety of useful ways; the role of the truly uncommon man in this or in any age is unique. A special word concerning his status is in order:

All human accomplishments are important in varying degree, but the achievements of a limited few have been very great indeed. This is to be expected, for in any field of endeavor, some will lead and some will follow; some will succeed conspicuously, some moderately, others not at all. While all contribute to the common good, the few at the top of their respective fields contribute in an extraordinary degree, since great individual success is never attained without bringing a measure of that success to many others.

Individual accomplishment marks the beginning of a chain reaction extending its influences far and wide; it is a catalyst which awakens desire in others and crystallizes effort which might otherwise lie dormant.

Henry Ford's genius for mass production created wonders in terms of employment, profit, and enjoyment for millions of people. The impact of Albert Einstein upon scientists and laymen alike the world over has been profound; Kreisler's extraordinary mastery of the violin has brought enjoyment to millions.

Try as we will, we can create no synthetic genius, no composite leader. Men are *not* interchangeable parts like so many pinion gears or carburetors; genius, as John Adams said, is bestowed "imperiously" by nature upon an individual. And behind every advance of the human race is a germ of creation growing in the mind of some lone individual, an individual whose dreams waken him in the night while others lie contentedly asleep. It is he who is the indispensable man.

With all our technical advances, dreams are not yet machine made and cannot be produced by crash programs. They cannot be stockpiled, prefabricated, or improvised. They remain one of the most characteristic symptoms of human aspiration and one of the activities which is most exclusively the province of the individual.

By dreams, of course, we mean creative genius, and the task in science, in business, in education, and in every other phase of human activity is to develop and preserve within our institutions this priceless human quality. Unless we can do so, the problem we will bequeath to our successors will be a dismal legacy indeed.

THE
EXECUTIVE
FUNCTION

Discussions of the executive function frequently suffer through lack of suitable definition. The term "executive" itself is loose and indefinite, for, while no one is in doubt as to the function of a physician, a boiler engineer, or a barber *, an executive to most people is not much more than a name, and I doubt that there is any field of activity referred to so often and understood so little.

An examination of the definition in eminent and very heavy dictionaries leads one to conclude that no definition is good and some are very bad indeed. The subject is dismissed with vague references to the executive phase of government, or by the helpful comment that an executive is "any person doing executive work." Of business executives as such, there is scarcely a word.

* All three of whom must, in most states, pass tests by licensing authorities before practicing their art.

The Bureau of the Census is even less enlightening, for it does not attempt a suitable classification, and we do not even know how many "executives" there really are. There is one category which the Bureau calls "managers, officials and proprietors," in which it lists some six million persons as "gainfully employed" and refers somewhat sadly to an additional one hundred thousand who are "looking for work." But I doubt that the six million managers, officials, and proprietors are all executives in the sense that corporations regard that function.

The criteria for high performance in the executive field are equally vague. Some months ago, I had some visitors from *Fortune* magazine who were conducting a study on the character traits most likely to be found in a good executive. Although we must have discussed the subject for two or three hours, I was unable to offer any formula which seemed to me to be generally applicable. I am afraid my visitors left with a keen sense of disappointment, and I am not sure to this day whether this arose from a reluctant agreement with my viewpoint or was a reflection on my inability to answer what, for them, was a very simple question.

Some seventy-five corporation executives interviewed by *Fortune*'s reporters during the course of this study found little common ground and came closest to a consensus in their replies to a question as to which of fourteen familiar character traits* they deemed "indispensable." A third of the respondents held "all" to be, while the rest simply rated some more so than others. Most recitals of executive virtues sound, as a matter of fact, rather like the McGuffey Readers or those little cards which pop out of penny scales certifying that the customer is loyal, trustworthy, kind, honest, generous, and weighs 198 pounds. The difficulty is that we have seen men who have all of these characteristics, but who would never make good executives. Other men might have a relatively poorer score in certain categories, but would, in their own way, be among the best. People are people and will, I suspect, continue to confound all efforts to classify them in neat little pigeonholes.

What makes a good executive good? I confess that I find that a most difficult question and, with all due respect, I doubt that many would find it very much easier.

In other fields of endeavor, talent can be recog-

---

* Judgment; initiative; integrity; foresight; energy-drive; human-relations skill; decisiveness; dependability; emotional calm; fairness; ambition; dedication; objectivity; cooperation.

nized readily and quickly. We have only to listen to a pianist, examine the work of an artist, or observe an actress on the stage to determine whether or not they are of outstanding rank. In other fields, there are recognized standards to aid judgment. A lawyer must pass a bar examination, a surgeon can refer you to his diploma from the American College, a ball player's batting average is published in the newspapers daily. Among executives, we can recognize competence only after long periods of observation and, even then, there are sometimes large differences of opinion. How much more difficult it is to appraise potential in advance! In this area, I am sure we have all made bad guesses, even with candidates who appeared highly promising.

It seems to me that the attributes which make a successful executive are found more than anywhere else in the intangibles. A job analysis, useful enough in other areas, falls down completely in appraising executive potential, for the duties defy classification or description.

I remember with some embarrassment a visit paid me some years ago by a young lady who was preparing a college thesis on management duties. The first thing she asked was what did I do all day.

That was a fair question, but I am afraid the difficulty I had in answering it put me at the bottom of the class. The more I thought about it, the more I was impressed by the fact that, in the executive area, there is no fixed procedure, no precise pattern, no yardstick of performance which can be counted and measured.

What *did* I do in any given day? An electrician or a painter could have given a ready answer; so, presumably, could a burglar, but certainly I could not and the stature of executives in the mind of my young visitor was not enhanced. Perhaps some could do better than I, but I am inclined to doubt it and to conclude that the difficulty of description merely emphasizes the imponderables which make up the executive's daily chores.

Most studies agree that an essential quality is "leadership," and I have no doubt that leadership is, in fact, an important executive attribute. But here again, we betray the limitations of our vocabulary for, while leadership is important, I am not at all sure that it is more than a small fraction of the answer. An articulate clergyman, for example, may be an able leader of ethical thought, or a soldier may exercise great leadership entirely through courage and personal example. Neither of them need necessarily have executive talent as we conceive it.

Judgment is important. Vision is undoubtedly essential. And we could exhaust our list of virtues without reaching the core of the problem. For I have known men with leadership, with judgment, with vision, who were not in any sense of the word good executives.

The best that I can offer is to say that the basic requirement of executive capacity is the ability to create a harmonious whole out of what the academic world calls dissimilar disciplines. This is a fancy way of saying that an executive is good when he can make a smoothly functioning team out of people with the many different skills required in the operation of a modern business. His most important function is to reconcile, to coordinate, to compromise, and to appraise the various viewpoints and talents under his direction to the end that each individual contributes his full measure to the business at hand.

Perhaps the best analogy to an executive's job is that of the symphony conductor under whose hand a hundred or so highly specialized and very different talents become a single effort of great effectiveness. No conductor can play every musical instrument and no more can an executive be skilled in every talent he is called upon to supervise. There was a time when the boss prided himself on personal experience with every job in the shop. If this view ever had merit, it has long since become entirely unrealistic. Today, specific skill in any given field becomes less and less important as the executive advances through successive levels of responsibility. Today, for example, there are thousands of people in the Du Pont Company whose expertness in their special fields I can regard only with awe and admiration. And to make the sad cycle complete, I have been out of touch with my own field of chemical engineering for so long that I cannot even talk on equal terms with the young men of that profession.

One thought that I passed along to my friends from *Fortune* seemed constructive to me, but I fear that they were not impressed. This was an observation that, while executive ability cannot be catalogued or measured, it can almost invariably be recognized. I cannot say what there is about extraordinary ability which projects itself so unmistakably, but somehow it does, transcending any personal differences and defying all preconceptions.

It is my principal task to recommend candidates for our important managerial posts. I have had to do that many times and have always accompanied my recommendations with a recital of the man's virtues, much, I am afraid, in the McGuffey Reader style. I frequently encounter from my associates violent disagreement over some particular virtue which I have emphasized, but, when it comes to an over-all judgment of the man and his suitability for the post at hand, it is a very rare circumstance when the choice is not unanimous.

Achievement in the executive field is much less spectacular than comparable success in many of the professions—the scientist, for example, who wins the Nobel Prize, the headline name who is elected governor, the skillful politician, the articulate college president. In fact, the more effective an executive, the more his own identity and personality blend into the background of his organization. Here is a queer paradox. The more able the man, the less he stands out, the greater his relative anonymity outside his own immediate circle.

So, as we pass more and more away from special, measurable skills into the less definable intangible talents, it becomes clear that the selection of executives becomes more of an art and less of a science.

We must rely in large measure on intuition and hope and pray that our candidate's performance will reflect our wisdom rather than our incompetence.

I am sure that all organizations have made mistakes in judgment of personnel and that the equities are sometimes compromised if not outraged by such errors. On the other side, however, I can't remember more than a very small handful of people whom I would say had not gotten their just deserts in terms of their abilities. I have worked at all levels of the Du Pont Company in 36-odd years, and I know a great many people, from wage-roll workers up. And the cases in which someone suffered an injustice are nearly negligible.

It may take time—I've often seen instances in which a man who was ready for a promotion had to wait two or three years, or perhaps four or five years, before it came. The realities of the situation were such that it couldn't be given to him at the instant in which he was ready for it. But given time he got there.

This time lag produces a certain amount of frustration, to be sure. There have been men who lost patience and left the company because they were unwilling to stay out the race. And it is true that the road to upper management has its detours, its rough spots, and its potholes.

But assuming that the time factor did not raise insuperable barriers, I know few whose talents have been slighted or by-passed. I would say that far more have been promoted who have not made the grade than have failed to reach positions within their capacity. In looking at promotions and advances over a long period of time, I think we've made more errors of commission than we have of omission.

It would be comforting, I suppose, if you could put your candidate on a scale of competence and weigh his worth as you might his avoirdupois. There have been a great many efforts to devise tests and formulae which would be definitive in gauging human capabilities. I am not persuaded that any of them are entirely successful. Indeed, we should, I think, take comfort in the fact that there are some remaining areas of life immune to quantitative analysis.

Tests invariably reflect a concern for "adjustment." The other day, I chose one of the standard psychological testing sheets used so widely now in personnel work and applied it to a rare and highly individualistic American—Benjamin Franklin. Based on what we know of Franklin's character, I could only conclude that he would have had bad luck winning a place for himself today if he were judged on these standards.

Some of the questions are highly esoteric. One, for example, asks, "Do you daydream?" Ben, I am afraid, did—often. An affirmative answer would merit a poor score on the test, although Franklin's daydreams brought useful results in fields ranging from political science to bifocal spectacles.

"Are you impatient?" another question reads. Ben was—at least, he was impatient with conditions he found unsatisfactory and equally so with the people he thought responsible. "Are you more entertained by books than by companions?" I would guess that he was, at least by some books than by some companions. The response would be held against him, presumably on the theory that it is better to be gregarious than to be well informed. On some questions, I must concede I was unable to find any answer. Did he, for example, "get hungry suddenly with a quick pang?" I don't know, nor am I sure what that question is supposed to tell us.

My guess is, too, that Charles Goodyear and Elias Howe would have been rated as impractical dreamers, and Thomas Edison, with a history of insomnia and carelessness in dress, might well have been regarded by the modern personnel manager as an undesirable risk.

It seems to me somehow offensive to human dignity to rely upon psychological testing bureaus in forming our personal judgments. Most such procedures assume a standard or a personality pattern against which candidates can be calibrated, and a set of job specifications which tend to give a fixed rigid image of the nominee.

I don't like these assumptions, nor do I like precise job descriptions. Any two able people to whom you might entrust a major assignment could quite conceivably achieve equally admirable results by diametrically opposed methods. Once management begins writing prescriptions, it must be held responsible if the patient dies.

Anything which inhibits the individual in expressing his own particular personality serves to deprive the organization of initiative. Our problem is to keep alive the powerful stimulant of individual thought at all levels and in every phase of our effort. Unless we do, we run the risk of making a displaced person out of the Man with the Big Idea.

Difficulties of interpretation in the areas of "testing" and "establishing criteria" have, from time to time, gotten me into trouble with my academic friends, many of whom are devoting quite distinguished careers to teaching "principles of management." Actually, I would say they are teaching a background for managerial work, not management itself. I have often commented to the effect that the most critical qualification of the manager, or executive if you will, is the ability to get along with people. I rather doubt that a concern for people is something which can be learned in school like logarithms or French verbs, but by this I do not discount the many facets of administrative procedure which can be taught. Tools and techniques can be acquired; the human qualities which go beyond them can, I am afraid, be given to us only by our genes and chromosomes.

As I have noted elsewhere, there is a close analogy between good management and good manners. By manners, I do not mean the enshrinement of Emily Post or of knowing the right fork to use. Good manners are built on consideration, on unselfishness, and on genuine and unfailing courtesy. The man who is a jolly tinker to those whom he seeks to impress, but who shouts at his wife or his secretary has no manners whatever, but only a purely superficial veneer. Not for very long will he be able to

inspire the confidence, the trust, and the cooperation of his people.

I incline strongly, therefore, to the belief that
the more fundamental equipment of the executive
is the result of what he has learned over long years
of experience through the age-old process of trial
and error.

We should also take note of the fact that few
people start out in life with the idea of becoming
executives. Most of us begin our careers in some
specialized field, perhaps science or finance or law,
and, as young men, our hopes and aspirations are
bound up in the pursuit of that chosen vocation.
Executive responsibility comes later in life, almost
wholly as a result of the office seeking the man.
Often, it comes as a complete surprise. That is as it
should be, for while there are always volunteers for
better jobs, the raised hand is rarely a satisfactory
guide.

I am aware of the fact that there are in this
country something over a hundred professional
schools of business and some four hundred 4-year
colleges which permit students to concentrate their
efforts towards this field—business administration
majors, as a matter of fact, make up a group second
only to teachers in the number of annual graduates.

Such training, while valuable as groundwork, does not make executives. I do not say that the school of business is without its place; I would be as reluctant to say that as I would be to say that science cannot be taught. But the point I wish to make is this: That, in teaching any discipline, the most that can be done is to show the student a kit of tools and to impart to him the rudiments of their use. He may use them well, or he may use them badly—which way he uses them is less a matter of his education than of his outlook and adaptability.

There are many matters pertaining to business which one can teach in a classroom. The thing which bothers me is the feeling that a man can be taught to be an executive in a classroom. This I don't think can be done—it is not a matter of technical knowledge in economics or in labor relations. It's a matter of human sympathy and human understanding: Men's qualifications to reach high positions are based not so much on their technical competence or job know-how as on what kind of people they are. Contrary to accepted thought, the good manager manages quite as much with his heart as with his head; quite as much with instinct and intuition as with precise formulae.

So I am afraid that the development and appraisal of executive talent cannot be done in our colleges, but must await experience in the practical realm of business operation. Our bright young men will start as chemists, salesmen, and accountants and it is up to us—the present generation of executives—to identify the capacities and the potential performance which will permit intelligent selection of our successors.

There is, of course, nothing unusual about the concept of learning while on the job, and certainly it is not peculiar to the business field. The idea of a university, as Newman and various others have described it, is simply that of a catalogue which sets forth the areas of human thought and indicates the avenues through which each may be explored. After that, it is up to the individual. He may go as far along the road as his personal tastes and capacities dictate.

How many of us, in any field or in a general sense, can look back upon the day we became college graduates and say that, on that day, we were educated people? I am sure I cannot, and I know few who can. An education is not a completed edifice developed in a few semesters of study and delivered with our diploma—it is a synthesis built up over years of exposure and experience. How well we are educated, it seems to me, is simply a matter of how well we have adjusted ourselves to our lives and our environment, whether we have enlarged our horizons or been content to vegetate.

Most, if not all, of the interests which broaden and enrich our lives culturally are developed long after we have left college. One of my own interests is Roman history, yet, at graduation, I could recognize neither Tacitus nor Diocletian. My fancy for serious music was not developed in college; in those days, I listened respectfully to "Whispering" and "Avalon," like everyone else. I've been running a hard race for many years against the list of books and authors I hope eventually to know; I caught up with Thackeray only a year or so ago.

Suppose that you have a course to give in English Literature. What is it that you want to leave in your students' minds? You don't look for them to become experts on Shakespeare, or Charlotte Brontë, or Dickens, or Scott. What you want to leave with them, it seems to me, is the conviction that the field of belles lettres is worth exploring. You provide them with some examples demonstrating the richness of the field and hope that they will find pleasure and inspiration in pursuing it throughout their lives.

You can teach a man the sciences, but you cannot make him a scientist. You can teach him engineering, but you cannot make him an engineer. And in exactly the same way, you can teach him executive procedures, but you can't make him an executive.

BUSINESS STEREOTYPES: OLD AND NEW

Not long ago, a young English professor of my acquaintance was telling me about a collection of letters written by a Boston businessman back in the 1840's. He expressed amazement that this gentleman and some of his commercial confreres had been members of a club which had numbered among its principal ornaments Mr. Ralph Waldo Emerson.

"Imagine Emerson hobnobbing with business people," he remarked morosely.

Well, I don't know. I have a feeling that Mr. Emerson might have done worse, and I get a little weary of the assumption that business people are quite the Philistines which many seem to think. For some reason, we tend to think of various callings in terms of rigid stereotypes. The businessman comes on stage as an uncouth character who scoffs at all cultural pretensions and who will stop at nothing to fill his pockets. It's not a pleasant concept, and it is not any closer to the truth than our other stereotypes: The absent-minded professor, or the drunken reporter, the long-haired musician, the interfering mother-in-law, or the plumber who arrives without his tools.

I've known a great many business people. My own impression is that it would be as hard to crystalize a "typical" example out of the lot as it would be to find a wholly representative sports editor, guitar player, or geologist. And just as pointless. I know businessmen who are professionally single minded and are dull companions outside their narrow field of interest. I know others whose minds range broadly through literature, music, history, painting and all the related disciplines, with a scholarship which would qualify them for high places on any university faculty.

Business generally is made up of people with all kinds of backgrounds, all kinds of motivations, and all kinds of tastes, just as in any other form of human endeavor. Business, in one way or another, involves something over three-fourths of us, and even within a given business unit we find people of every conceivable type.

Business, in short, is not made up of charts and credit balances, but of perfectly normal and, we hope, perfectly rational human beings. I find it hard to believe that *all* its people would be drawn from either the morally weak or the culturally disenfranchised. I am inclined to think that the group of people comprising business management has pretty much the same proportion of good, bad, and indifferent qualities as any other. Men elect to enter the field of business just as they may choose some other vocation—the law, or journalism, or the clergy, or teaching—sometimes through a leaning or predilection, often through pure circumstance.

If we can concede that people in the main have decent, honorable, and reasonable standards of taste and behavior, I think we can say that those in the business world average out at about the same level as any other. Any disfigurement which society may suffer will come from man himself, not from any given profession or vocation.

In the library of literature dealing with business, flattering portraits are very rare. American novels such as Howells' *Silas Lapham*, John Dos Passos' *U. S. A.*, Upton Sinclair's *The Jungle*, and Dreiser's *The Titan* leave a highly unrealistic impression of the business environment, particularly under the conditions prevailing today. And unfortunately fully contemporary efforts such as *Executive Suite, The Big Business Look, A Really Sincere Guy,* and *The Spiked Heel* have done little to improve understanding.

The businessman is a victim, I am afraid, of his poor press, for the public seems to weigh him on a different set of scales than it uses elsewhere, whether it is assessing moral fiber or cultural deficiencies. There are, of course, men who enter the business world and become so engrossed in immediate affairs that they ignore all else. They live in narrow cells of their own making; the world looks at them and deplores their lack of culture. But this process is by no means exclusive to business; we see it at work in every other element of life. We see professors of history with few interests outside their own. We see artists indifferent to everything but their canvases; physicians who are lost outside their medical specialty; lawyers unlearned in all save law.

Yet even between professions, communications are made difficult by mutual preconceptions. Business people sometimes think of professors as starry-eyed dreamers, while professors not infrequently regard a reasonably literate businessman as a curiosity. I once met a classical historian who was rather stunned when he learned of my enthusiasm for Roman history and familiarity with Gibbon.

Too often, I fear, we criticize the one-dimensional businessman while somehow finding excuses or even applause for the single-minded professor or artist or scientist. Yet I find it hard to differentiate. The narrow cell is as spiritually cramped whether it is an office, a laboratory, a studio, or a classroom.

Is there anything about the business process itself to make a difference? I cannot agree that there is. I cannot see that there is anything to make commercial institutions less worthy or less desirable or less ennobling of their participants than other institutions or other professions. If we were called upon to recreate a primitive society on a desert island, with each of us contributing his special skill to the community enterprise, there would be no reason to regard the man who made shoes in a less useful or less flattering light than the man who made poetry or sermons, or even laws. The fact that we today identify shoes as a commercial venture and others as cultural or spiritual or professional does not change the essential nature of any.

There is, of course, the theory that we in this century are burdened with the guilt of previous generations and that the folk image of the businessman * today is dictated by the ghosts of the Robber Barons. It is true that impressions, like heirlooms, have an astonishing and often unfortunate longevity. We inherit ideas from our parents who may well have acquired them from their own parents. And as with many heirlooms, they are more notable for venerability than for value.

Perhaps this intransigence of thought has helped to perpetuate the indestructible legend which cast the businessman of the past century as a pirate in mutton-chop whiskers. A tough operator, the legend insists, ruthlessly destroying competition, fleecing his customers, exploiting his employees.

Personally, I have my doubts. Manners and customs have changed in business as they have elsewhere, but fundamentals have not. Today, we know that business institutions succeed by the process of providing a useful service, keeping their customers satisfied and by maintaining a high level of employee morale.

I conclude that somewhere along the line the story has been subjected to some embellishment. Very possibly the business types who live in sharp-

* Perhaps I should take note here of Emerson's comment that there is no such thing as a businessman, but only a man in business.

est memory were the extreme cases, representing a tiny minority of the business community. The more typical examples would probably be pretty much like their grandsons today, differing only as the character of their times differed from our own.

Unquestionably, the code prevailing in the late Nineteenth Century was one influenced by a frontier economy and a picturesque, self-seeking exuberance. It was an age of great individual opportunity when men of little education and of small cultural background could and did acquire large fortunes. If some conducted themselves with less gentility and circumspection, there is little to indicate that the public conscience was outraged.

It should be remembered, also, that business operations of that era were very largely one-man enterprises in which the business and the man could scarcely be differentiated. Mr. Scrooge, answering only to himself, could do pretty much as he liked, and if his business suffered as a result, it was of little concern to others. The day had not yet come when corporations would have a life beyond the tenure of any individual and come to represent not only a multiple proprietorship, but a multiple responsibility. The 1890 business titan, heading up his own works, was exposed but little to the sobering thought that, while he would pass along, the institution would endure.

Some of our modern critics, while rebuking the memory of Jim Fisk and Jay Gould, are sufficiently tolerant to applaud the "new type" of executive. I am afraid that I find this notion equally as wearisome as the legend of the toolless plumber. It is presented as though, by some process of sexless eugenics, the bull terriors and bloodhounds of the business past had been cross-bred to produce a race of kindly and socially conscious poodles. I have never been able to accept this concept. It seems to me that men will always reflect the environment in which they live and will respond to its pressures, its ideals, and its customs in much the same way. As society develops and grows both spiritually and materially, the individuals comprising it will, on the average, grow and develop with it in business or any other field.

One of the most difficult tasks of the historian, of course, is to evaluate an era or an individual of long ago in valid terms. Almost always our value judgments are weighted by the mores and the standards of our own day rather than those of some bygone period. It is necessary, therefore, to winnow out the deciduous values which change with the times before rendering judgment on the fundamentals which endure.

The ground rules of behavior have a way of changing every generation or so and the ethical fashions in vogue at any one time are sometimes as whimsical as fashions in dress or home decoration. Once we get beyond the Ten Commandments, it is rather difficult to apply absolute standards in the area of public morals.

If, by modern standards, the conduct of early business people is open to any question, criticism can with equal validity be directed at many other areas of activity. Both Washington and Jefferson, highly moral men, were slave owners following a practice which, while distasteful to us, was generally accepted in their day. Lincoln, revered by all of us, saw nothing wrong with wangling a place on Grant's staff for his young son, explaining that he "wouldn't want him to serve in the ranks." No one complained, but imagine such an incident today!

Moral standards to a large extent parallel growth and progress of the economy. Peoples constantly in peril of starvation exhibit an indifference to human life and suffering shocking to more fortunate races. The Eskimo leads his elderly parent out on the ice with stoic calm; the desert nomad sells his daughters into slavery simply as a way of survival.

In the frontier society of a hundred years ago, with a technology barely able to meet subsistance needs, people lived by a code which was conditioned by the realities of the day. The important thing is that we avoid retrospective judgments—that we judge the past by its own rule book and not ours. And, equally important, to exclude from present-day thought those old-time throwbacks which, in modern circumstances, are as outmoded as a beaver hat.

THE GREAT
AMERICAN
PARADOX

I

I cannot present myself as an authority on taxation except possibly in that same melancholy sense in which a pedestrian is an authority on taxicabs because one has knocked him down. I am no expert on budgetary matters and could not possibly suggest how much money it is wise for our government to spend under a given set of circumstances. I do not know what the average Federal tax rate should be. I will register my personal opinion that it is very high, but I am echoing here, of course, the cries of misery heard from taxpayers throughout recorded history. When the income tax amendment was first adopted in 1913, a married man earning $10,000 a year was required to pay a Federal tax of $60. I understand that even then there were bitter complaints. No one has ever devised a painless method for levying taxes, and it is doubtful that the collector will ever be welcomed, whatever the country, whatever the era.

It seems clear that government expenditures must remain high, perhaps for the foreseeable future, and surely no one can take issue with expenditures assuring the country's defense, whatever they may be. It is, however, simple prudence to levy taxes in such a way as to render the least damage to our economy, for, without a dynamic industry, it is difficult to visualize an adequate defense program, whatever the tax rate. Here, of course, there is much room for debate, but it seems to me that the greatest threat to industry, and to the aggressive drive of our people, lies in our steeply progressive system of taxes on personal income.

Progressive income taxes can be attacked on many grounds. I share the concern of most business men as to the reduced availability of venture capital, for taxes eliminate the source which once supported the would-be entrepreneur. I share the concern of many as to the effect of steeply progressive taxes on personal incentive and the loss to our country inherent in a lower level of individual effort and accomplishment.

Hazardous as these consequences may be, it seems

to me that the most serious question to be raised about the present tax system is not so much in the area of economics or politics, but in the field of morals.

I often think how confused a picture this age of ours will present to a future historian looking back with all the erudition of hindsight. What an astonishing paradox we will present: We set extraordinary standards of achievement and accord it great popular acclaim. No culture and no nation, in fact, has ever shown such admiration for distinction in so wide a variety of interests.

Critics passing future judgments may snort that our veneration of movie starlets, television personalities, and hard-hitting outfielders brands us as a decadent race, but I wouldn't agree. Much as we admire Miss Marilyn Monroe, Mr. Ted Williams, or Mr. Jackie Gleason, and great as is our annual furore over bathing beauties, marble champions, prize heifers, and Miss Rheingold, our accolades encompass leaders in all fields in the cultural, the spiritual, the scientific, and even the business areas. We have honors and applause for Eugene Ormandy, for Jonas Salk, for Bishop Sheen and Norman Vincent Peale, for James Bryant Conant, for Marian Anderson and for Andrew Wyeth. We have fame to bestow upon singers of arias and singers of blues, makers of automobiles and makers of roll-a-hoops, writers of poetry and writers of insurance, heads of state and heads of coaching, jockeys of disc and jockeys of horse.

No, the admiration of the American people for achievement in any field is obvious and cannot be gainsaid. Our paradox lies in the fact that, when the rewards of achievement are paid in dollars rather than in honors or cheers, we say "no, no!" and tax most of them away. We admire success, but penalize the successful; we admire talent, but penalize the talented; we admire initiative, yet penalize the initiator; we admire leadership, yet we penalize our leaders. Cheers and applause, yes! Financial reward, no!

For a dozen years or so, we have somehow rationalized the strange thesis that minority rights applicable to the talented and successful could, if their compensation were financial, be safely abrogated. I am afraid that the issue has been drawn too often along political rather than moral lines. Politically, the talented and successful people of America —despite their public appeal—represent a minority group with few champions. As a result the evil of confiscatory taxes has, like vice, been first endured and

ultimately embraced regardless of the wrong it im-
poses, regardless of the threat it poses to the future.

Too little thought has been given, I am afraid,
to the moral implications of taxing away 90 per cent
of one man's earnings to make another's burden
seem less unpalatable. If there is any equity at all
in this approach, I have yet to hear anyone venture
to expound it and I suspect that few would relish
the role in which espousal would cast them.

If the victims of our high tax rates were only
those in the top brackets, the financial effects could
perhaps be endured, painful though they might be
to present company. But morally, the imposition
and the acceptance of an evil so grossly discriminatory against one element of society cannot fail to
have its effect upon every element. And the influence broadly upon the moral fiber of the nation,
present and future, cannot fail to be profound.

Since the very beginning, Americans have held
fast to a set of moral principles which have served
them well. Implicit in the tradition of individual
freedom is a fierce independence and a disposition
toward sturdy self-reliance. With the flame of liberty burning bright, men have been inspired to scale
such heights as their abilities would permit and
to assume, with success, a full share of their responsi-

bilities and obligations, not only to their own enterprises, but to their neighbors and to the nation itself.

I cannot help but feel that the effect of our present tax philosophy upon this structure will be as
sweeping as it is destructive. In our exercise of the
democratic principle, we decided that there were
certain functions that could best be performed by
a central government, and we have given that government permission to levy taxes upon us to the extent necessary to perform those functions.

The fact remains that we are very much nearer a
system of proportional taxation, or what the church
used to call tithing, than any of us think. Many
studies exist, made by eminent economists, that
show that when the overall tax bill is 25 per cent,
every citizen, rich or poor, is paying in taxes very
nearly that percentage of his own income. The
trouble is that he does not know it, for the largest
part of the bill has been concealed from him, and he
goes on blithely thinking that the cost of government is being paid by his neighbor.

Our tax bill today is about 25 per cent of the value
of the country's entire productive effort, and yet we
are asked to believe that the greater part of that
huge bill is collected from a handful of wealthy
people and large corporations. Many studies have

been made which show quite clearly that this is not the case. The aggregate amount of personal income taxes in excess of 25 per cent of gross income, for example, represents about $3 billion, or some 4½ per cent of total tax revenues. And if those in the $50,000 and up bracket were stripped completely of all income, the result would scarcely net enough to operate our federal government for a single day.

Only to a negligible extent can the steeply progressive aspect of personal income tax be regarded as a justifiable exercise of the revenue function. It has become rather a denial of the principle of high reward for high accomplishment, and hence a bow to the Marxian theory "From everyone according to his ability to everyone according to his need."

In a previous chapter, I have emphasized incentives and rewards and the part they play in bringing out the greatest effort and the highest talent of the average individual. For many generations, this country, operating under the free society established by our Constitution, has held fast to this principle. The experiment has been successful beyond our wildest imaginings and has brought us to our present high stature among the nations of the world.

Our large population creates tempting mass mar-

kets for the successful entrepreneur, but some
nations outnumber us and many are not far behind.
We have a large territory—at the beginning, rich
and unexplored—but here again we are not unique.

We can, of course, take great pride in the character and mental capacity of our citizens, but again I
doubt that we are in any way exceptional. I suspect
that the inherent mental ability of the average
American does not differ substantially from that of
the average Englishman, the average mid-European,
or the average Russian.

I think it is safe to say that the human raw material available to this country, expressed in terms
of mental capacity, is not substantially different from
the equivalent in any other nation. What we have
done is to increase the fruitfulness of our spiritual
soil by providing the fertilizer of incentive to each
of our citizens.

I have heard a good deal about the "peaceful economic warfare" vowed recently by Mr. Khrushchev
between his country and ours. I have heard many proposals as to the new role American business must
play in countering that offensive. It seems to me,
however, that the issue is basically a simple one.
Granted the premise that the average Russian is as
intelligent as his American counterpart, the ques-

tion becomes one of the economic system which will produce from a given population the most outstanding result. In the beginning, we chose a free society with individual incentives and rewards. Soviet Russia chose totalitarianism and the Marxian distrust of personal gain. Had those two systems been allowed to stand as originally conceived, there could be no possible doubt that the Russian economic offensive would fail.

In recent years, however, the Russians have come to realize the importance of personal rewards in inducing maximum effort and ingenuity in their people. Many observers of the Russian scene report the adoption of rewards and incentives throughout the industrial and educational fields. Sometimes these rewards take forms which are strange to us, but there can be no question at all that they are effective.

I have heard the report recently that a Russian professor of the highest rank, in a calling traditionally marked by low pay scales, is now paid the equivalent of $30,000 a year at the official rate of exchange and, in addition, is given relatively excellent housing accommodations, the use of an automobile, a summer home, and numerous other fringe benefits. I was somewhat startled to compute that this is just about equivalent to my own compensation from the Du Pont Company after applicable federal and state income taxes.

It seems quite clear that if financial rewards in the two countries are examined quantitatively, the Russians are not far behind us. What troubles me is to note that at the very time the Soviets are embracing our principle of incentive and show signs of benefiting thereby, we ourselves seem intent upon abandoning it.

In an experiment lasting over many generations, we have proved conclusively that a free society with incentives and rewards geared to personal accomplishment will produce a nation whose strength is second to none. The Russians give signs of having learned that lesson also. Whatever form economic warfare with Russia may take, I feel certain we can win only if we return to the principles which have brought us to our present high stature. If we do not, the battle will be a difficult one indeed.

II

By and large there is little real difference between the major problems of a business organization and the problems of most other organizations. In the area of compensation, however, there is an important difference. The principal incentives of the business world are financial, and for that reason the impact of high personal taxes falls most heavily upon the business unit.

To discuss the present and future of business management without reference to current tax laws is like planning your six-year-old's college career while neglecting to send him to school—it is to disregard factors which a generation hence may have far-reaching implications. And it is obviously with the future, not the present, that we should concern ourselves.

The business executive who talks about the threat to his organization posed by high personal income taxes exposes himself to all manner of indignant comment which questions his veracity, his sincerity, and his patriotism.

To anticipate as much rebuttal as I can, let me register this concession in advance: I do not believe that the *present* generation of management is rendered less determined or less dedicated in its efforts by current tax policies. Out of every dollar I was paid by the Du Pont Company last year, I was able to preserve for my own use perhaps 9 cents, yet I work just as hard, and I hope just as effectively, as

I would if my gross and net compensation were equal. I am sure that the same applies to each of my associates.

The reason is, of course, that by the time anyone reaches a position of authority or responsibility he acquires a different set of motivations than that which pushed him in his earlier years—loyalty takes over, or obligation, or perhaps, as has been suggested rather unkindly, conditioned reflex. I see frequently in the reports of stockholder meetings the statement that, if executive compensation were not so high as it is, there would be danger of losing existing management to other businesses or to other professions. I doubt very much that those statements are fully justified.

My concern is not with those in management today, but with the caliber of men who will be managing our business enterprises twenty-five or fifty years from now. How can we assure competence and vigor throughout our business organizations in the face of greatly weakened financial incentives? On the answer to that question depends much of the country's future, not only as an industrial producer, but as a world power.

While the present momentum will probably carry through the next generation, or even the one after that, sooner or later the difficult road to high competence will seem less worth the effort.

Too often, discussions of financial incentive lead to the assumption that only top-level people are involved or affected. This is far from true: Incentives are largely relative and actually if compensation is to provide incentive, the scale must be calibrated from the bottom up rather than from the top down, with a sufficient differential between one level and the next to make promotion attractive.

Gross remuneration serves as a beacon light to others. In our company, for example, we have felt it wise to maintain a fairly constant percentage of increase in pay for each upward step in the ladder of advancement. In recent years, this has, of course, been difficult to do in terms of net income, no matter how high the gross figure. In our efforts to enhance the attractiveness of the next step ahead, we have occasionally encountered criticism because the before-tax compensation at the upper levels appeared to be unduly high. The criticisms frequently embrace the argument that the recipient must surrender a large share of his compensation to the government in taxes; therefore why pay it to him? I am afraid this is an attitude which the tax collector might view with alarm, but, at any rate, we have never accepted it—the point is that the high gross compensation is not nearly so important to the man getting it as it is to the fellow a step or two below! It is important primarily as an added facet of the incentive system.

Compensation at each level must be sufficiently greater to tempt the man below to make the climb. If we say an increase of 25 per cent, after taxes, for each rung of the ladder is reasonable, simple arithmetic pushes gross compensation at the top into stratospheric levels which do little more than arouse employee and stockholder indignation and make the incumbent wonder whether a take-home pay of 9 cents on the dollar is worth all the censure and abuse!

There is one disturbing indication already. I have said that a diminished financial reward seems to have little effect on the present executive group. Some of my associates have noted, however, that among the younger people, there are already signs indicating that promotion is a little less attractive than it used to be. Probably where it exists at present, this is not a rational or reasoned course, but simply a reflection of an attitude conditioned by the times. A college questionnaire a few years ago indicated that a majority of the graduating class placed "a modest income with security" as the pinnacle of aspiration.

Now security, I suppose, is the most universal, certainly the most worthy, of man's desires. He wishes it for himself, for his children, for his neighbors. I am sure everyone would agree that personal security is desirable, even essential for each of us and for the nation. It is not the goal, but the method of reaching it that is in question.

The theory that seems to have found wide acceptance today is that personal security is in some way a right, either of citizenship or of employment. As our society increases in complexity, as our organizations increase in size, the individual comes more and more to believe himself to be a small cog in a large machine, and so arrives at the conclusion that the machine itself in some way owes him not only a livelihood, but perpetual security as well.

To an extent, corporations can be said to have embraced some of this philosophy themselves, partly out of recognition of tax realities, partly because a corporation does, after all, reflect the attitudes of the public of which it is a part. Thus we see the corporation undertaking for its employees many of the functions once regarded as wholly personal.

The average employee of a modern corporation,

for example, looks forward to a pension paid in whole or in large part by his employer. He has an insurance policy bought at low rates through group coverage; if he falls ill, his medical expenses and hospitalization are underwritten in the same way; his personal savings are encouraged by a corporate contribution. Benefits of this kind are expected these days—the corporation bidding for manpower in the personnel market is obliged to meet competition with a program as good or better than that of other employers. Yet it does so, I am sure, with misgivings, for ideally each "benefit" is an intrusion upon the personal prerogatives of the employee. Someone not long ago asked me if the corporation were not becoming increasingly "paternalistic." With all due allowance for the ambiguous nature of the term, I could answer only that a state of "involuntary paternalism" does seem to exist.

To the extent that this trend continues, the effect upon the moral fabric must be an undesirable one. When a promising and able man in any field decides that security is sufficient, then the nation will be the poorer. If his decision becomes at all general, we are in trouble.

For it is that extra effort that wins, that has made American industry what it is today. The progress we have made has not been achieved by perfunctory or routine performance; it has come about because people have been inspired or induced to give everything they had to the task at hand—to do their best, and often a little more. The industrial miracle of America has come because our people have shown a capacity for accomplishment well beyond their rated potential. It must follow that anything which weakens that capacity will weaken our strength as a people and weaken us in the very way it is most difficult to remedy. A wasting illness can render a strong man weak and frail within a few days. But once stricken, his recovery, with the finest therapy and the most painstaking care, will take much longer and its success can never be guaranteed.

THE
OWNER'S EYE

The French peasant, a simple man with a nice natural feel for agrarian economics, has a saying that goes more or less like this: "The farm has no fertilizer half so good as the eye of the owner."

In the early days of American industry, the financial incentives motivating the proprietor of a business were as simple and declarative as those of the farmer in the dell. If his enterprise were successful, he prospered; if the business failed, he failed. Ownership and management were virtually synonymous and, by the sink-or-swim nature of the entrepreneurial process, the fortunes of the individual and the enterprise were inseparable.

I have no doubt that this principle contributed very greatly to the development of industry in this country. Owner-management such as was entailed in these early proprietorships remains as perhaps the most effective kind of human motivation. It combined challenge and inspiration with a touch of the lash implicit in failure.

Until the Twentieth Century, a business institution was run by the single hand of its owner and there was never any doubt about who was boss. Any authority held by a subordinate came only by the personal delegation of the proprietor or principal partner.

Today, the scale of business enterprise has revised our ideas of both ownership and management. As capital requirements have increased, ownership has become more and more diffused. Most large industrial companies today have a very large number of stockholders, and it is a rare thing for any one stockholder to own more than a small fraction of the total.

Management has similarly become plural rather than singular. Decision-making authority has become subdivided as organizations have grown. Management itself has become a profession more and more frequently dissociated from the concept of ownership.

The changes are natural and necessary. It is unfortunate, however, that, in devising new patterns, we drift ever farther away from the owner-management principle which was such a powerful influence for high performance. A personal stake in the progress and prosperity of the employer is the best guarantee I know for management devotion and the high flame of midnight oil.

We are strongly wedded to the owner-management idea in our company, and we are attempting as best we can to perpetuate it within the framework of a very large organization.

In the beginning when the company was a family business, owner-management was a natural condition and was the normal pattern of operation in most business ventures. Early in the present century when the old family partnership became a corporation, it was recognized that some way should be found to preserve the strength inherent in the ownership principle. The result was a bonus plan which was adopted in 1902 and which has been in continuous operation ever since. The important features of this plan are, first, that it is based wholly on earnings and, second, that awards are made in the form of common stock.

The result of the plan's operation at the outset was, of course, that the principal management people soon began to acquire a sense of participation. As their own share of the enterprise increased, the greater personal stake they began to have in the potential earnings provided the greatest possible incentive toward high performance. Over the years, it has worked out very successfully. Management at all levels has had a keen inducement to perform well, knowing that if earnings are high, the rewards will be commensurate and that, if they are low, the amount to be distributed is decreased.

More importantly, the stake in future earnings as participation increases gives them an eye to the future as well as to the present, and a concern for corporate growth and success far beyond their tenure in office.

In recent years, the ownership feature, particularly at the higher management levels, has been virtually nullified by the very high tax rates on income. The principle is maintained by making awards partially in stock, but, because the entire bonus is taxed as income, it is difficult for the average beneficiary, even in the middle brackets, to build up any very substantial equity.

I think there is no doubt that any company suffers a loss in vigor and vitality as owner-management is dissipated. I recall one anecdote which, it seems to me, illustrates the point. The late Lammot du Pont was once explaining the difficulties of maintaining the principle under the present tax system. A listener nodded in agreement, commenting that the hired manager, lacking a personal stake in the outcome, was likely to spend the company's money without exercise of due caution.

"That's not the point," said Lammot. "The danger is that he'll spend it with too *much* caution."

And, of course, he was right. People will assume risks with their own funds which they would not or could not dare when they are the stewards of other people's money. The owner is interested in the continuity and growth of his business; the employee on fixed salary is all too often interested in a safe, conservative performance during his working career.

There is perhaps no more significant change in the industrial scene than the impending general replacement of the venturesome owner-management spirit with ownership which becomes increasingly fragmentized in character. I have no quantitative analysis to offer, but I would guess that the average stockholder's stake in any single corporation is substantially less than the average of twenty-five years ago, despite a large increase in values. This is indicated clearly by the growth of the shareholder group in the typical corporation. And, as the ownership ranks enlarge and the relative stake declines, the element of personal concern in the affairs of the institution becomes more and more negligible.

An even more diffusing influence is the rise of institutional ownership where, by indirect means, millions of people have some financial interest in the American corporation. Here, I imply no disrespect of institutional shareholding, for it is essential and it is inevitable. The securities of American corporations are increasingly finding their way into the portfolios of mutual funds, of pension trusts, insurance companies, benevolent associations, and so forth, all of which are regulated institutions whose inclinations toward long risks are limited by both prudence and the law.

Necessarily, the institutional owner's connection with any one segment of its corporate holdings is indirect and impersonal. It does not have the permanent interest of one whose life is bound up with that of the corporation. So when we look for personal responsibility, we must come back to management as the institution whose interest is direct and intimate. The most effective way to preserve it, I think, is to find means of continuing the vital and energizing force of owner-management.

Obviously, ownership will continue to be diffuse. The capital requirements of the modern corporation and the trend of the times are such that no individual will own more than a small percentage. But so long as management is participating to some extent, the result should be good.

I have often been asked how ownership by a corporate executive of a few hundred or a few thousand shares of the millions represented in most large corporations can qualify under the classification of "owner-management." It is true that such holdings are a tiny fraction of the total, but the important thing, it seems to me, is not the percentage of outstanding shares held but the attitude which ownership of a substantial shareholding induces.

The precise stage at which this owner-attitude takes over varies, of course, with the individual. As good a definition as any, I think, is that men begin to think like owners when the income from their stock equals or exceeds the amount they may be looking forward to in retirement pay. It is then that the long-term view takes over and the individual begins to identify his own future interests with those of the corporation. We have a number of such interested individuals on our Board, and I can speak at firsthand of their devotion to the Company's long-range welfare, for in it they can recognize their own.

With the tax rates of recent years, accumulation of an ownership interest of any substance has become increasingly difficult. We have as a result given much thought to some way of retaining the spirit, if not the full measure, of the owner-management principle.

In the last year we have installed a new plan which we hope will, to some extent, recapture the main features of this principle. Under this plan a portion of the bonus award to an individual, instead of being paid him outright in cash or stock and thus subject to taxation as ordinary income, is retained by the company. In its place the individual receives over a period of years an amount equal to the dividends declared on one and one-half times the equivalent in common shares of the bonus which would otherwise have been awarded him. The undertaking to pay dividend equivalents runs to the eighty-fifth anniversary of the individual's birth, or his death, whichever is later, thus giving him an interest which extends well beyond his active period. He receives in addition a restricted stock option, replacing on exercise his dividend equivalents, so the possibility exists of converting his "limited" partnership to one that is permanent.

But whether he is a full or limited partner, employee's personal interest and that of the company become intimately connected. We hope by this method to reinstate some part of the owner-management concept which has been so successful in past years. I know of no other effort so likely to produce a satisfactory future.

THE
VANISHING
PHILANTHROPIST

In relegating the Genus Philanthropist to the status of the Great Auk and the Passenger Pigeon, government has marked for extinction one of the rarest and most useful of our economic institutions. Fortunately or unfortunately, men become philanthropists only when they have something to give away, and, if they never reach this state, they will in the main be unaware of their lost opportunities. The potential beneficiaries will receive some kind of largesse from other sources and, I suppose, will not be aware of any differences. But the institution, as it vanishes, will take with it something that is strong and significant and every American will share a loss larger than he will realize.

I grew up in mid-town Philadelphia within the shadow of a philanthropic institution which has long been a symbol of kindly benevolence and, from time to time, of bitter controversy. In any history of American philanthropy, both benevolence and controversy figure largely and Girard College must occupy an important and representative place. On the side of benevolence, this institution typifies the role of the private benefactor establishing, in furtherance of his own ideas, a monument to human charity. On the side of controversy, it emphasizes the fact that acts of private philanthropy do not always win immediate public favor and sometimes, by their very nature, are beyond popular support. If the designation of funds to charitable or welfare purposes were left entirely to popular vote then many of our institutions of great value, but of specialized appeal, would not exist.

Girard College where for many years my father was staff physician came into being by the bequest of Stephen Girard, an unregenerate individualist who, when he died in 1831, was reputed to be the richest man in America. His life and works represent one of the prime privileges of the free society: The right to amass a substantial competence and to dispose of it as one sees fit.

Girard was a poor orphan who came to America from France and made his way against great odds. He drove himself unremittingly toward building up a large fortune and, before he died, he stipulated the conditions of its disbursement so carefully and in such great detail that it is in litigation to this day.

The Girard will set up a fund of over 6 million dollars—an enormous sum in 1831—for the establishment of a college to be attended, free of charge, by "white male orphans of Philadelphia" who otherwise could not obtain an education. He made a great number of conditions, one being that religious services should have no part in the curriculum. Publication of the provisions caused a public outcry and, in the legal battle which followed, led by counsel as eminent as Daniel Webster, much effort was directed at setting the will aside.

The Supreme Court, however, upheld beyond question the citizen's right to bequeath his wealth as he wished and to make any provisions he desired. It was held that the act of benevolence is, by its very nature, a personal gesture, subject though it might be to personal whims and frailties or changing conditions which not infrequently present trustees a century hence with serious problems. (Girard's will is still being challenged on the grounds that the designation of "white male orphans" is discriminatory against Negroes.)

I hold no brief for either the wisdom or the propriety of Girard's will, nor would I argue the merits of binding posterity to a set of circumstances a century old. The point is clear, however, that, despite errors of judgment, despite mistakes, despite occasional foolishness, benefactions have flourished under our free institutions, with large benefit to the public good.

A vast enrichment of our culture has come about through those whose interest in some personal charitable venture has been reflected eventually in a public gain of much significance. Our major art galleries and collections, our museums, our symphony orchestras, our opera houses, our great parks and gardens have been made possible by large individual gifts—gifts not only of money, but of personal interest and dedication, given quite independently of popularity or public support, often in the face of it.

In the middle of the Nineteenth Century, for example, when there were few opportunities for women to get a college education. The majority opinion of the times, as summed up by a Reverend Dr. John Todd, held that "the normal structure, the physiology and the habit of thought of the female properly bans her from the halls of higher learning." But philanthropy steps in where politics

fears to tread. In 1861, Matthew Vassar, a Pough-
keepsie brewer, established the college which bears
his name today. He wrote that his interest in the
project was prompted by its "grandeur, its novelty
and its benignity," but, for whatever motives, the
deed was accomplished; female education was as-
sured; and public opinion, in time, followed along.
Dependent upon the cautious, vote-conscious leadership of the state, without the influence of those
strong enough and determined enough to swim
against the current, feminine education would have
been many years in the realizing.

Superficially, it might appear that the present tax
law which exempts contributions to the extent of
30 per cent of annual income gives sufficient lati-
tude to prospective donors. I have no doubt that it
has provided an incentive for the higher bracket tax
payer to give generously. Philanthropy on this basis
is purchasable at bargain basement prices, as agencies dependent upon gifts and contributions are
realistic enough to point out. A man with an annual
income of half a million dollars is able to disburse
among his various charitable interests up to $150,-
000. The premise that "the government will get it
anyhow," a view which might have troubled Good
King Wenceslaus, must nevertheless be counted a

factor in eleemosynary works of various character.

Whatever the immediate effects, however, the long-range result of the present law cannot help but be disastrous. It is plain that the consequence, if not the objective, of the prevailing tax philosophy in the United States must be to render the accumulation of large fortunes a virtual impossibility.

We approach the day—and it is not far distant— when really large beneficences are no longer available from the private donor. The loss to society will be severe.

Money in dribs and drabs may support and maintain institutions, but it doesn't establish them. "Founder's Day" invariably harks back to very substantial outlays of capital, guided and directed by personal zeal.

Many of our institutions of higher learning, for example, were established by private endowments and bequests of great magnitude, as their very names indicate: Vanderbilt; Carnegie; Armour; Cooper; Oberlin; Duke; Vassar; McGill; Goucher; Stevens; and a hundred more. M. I. T. received $20,000,000 from George Eastman; Chicago University was created from the ground up by John D. Rockefeller's personal efforts. The Harkness Memorial at Yale and the Sloan School of Industrial

Management at M. I. T. are typical of the many outstanding gifts for educational purposes.

The same thing applies in other fields. The Rockefeller contributions to medicine and other efforts related to the public welfare are estimated to have reached $550,000,000 (the equivalent of perhaps two billion today) which exceeds in itself the average annual total of all contributions for all purposes in this country prior to World War II. Andrew Carnegie whose impoverished youth left him highly respectful of book learning spent more than $60,-000,000 in 1901–1910 on libraries alone.*

With each gift has gone part of the character, part of the enthusiasm of the individual. These are assets which cannot, unfortunately, be replaced by passing the hat.

The scope and range of our giving is impressive. Whether we give a mite or a million, we give most generously and most gladly to those causes in which we have a special personal interest. With the freedom and the encouragement to pursue their own

* Carnegie was above personal credit-seeking. Carnegie libraries numbered in all 2,811, of which 1,946 were in the United States. Less than a third bore the donor's name—in Indiana alone there were 155, none of which are publicly identified with the giver.

fancies, men of wealth have been prompted to bestow upon the nation an extraordinary variety of philanthropic works reflecting their own tastes and enthusiasms and frequently things which are far ahead of their times.

Today's tax philosophy seems to follow the premise that government, not the individual, should make determinations regarding the needs of the public good. Under this theory, the state taxes away the funds once available for large gifts and parcels it out along such lines and under such conditions as it sees fit.

The tragic fact is that, under circumstances such as this, many of our most valuable cultural institutions would never have existed at all, or, if they continued under state auspices, would have acquired a character wholly different from that contemplated by the private donor.

The reason is obvious: The state, when it turns to such matters, must tailor its program to the general level. The public official necessarily deals with social problems in a dispassionate and impersonal way.

Private individuals, on the other hand, can and do undertake projects which would be impossible, or even improper, for the government to consider.

Pierre S. du Pont, for example, created at Longwood Gardens in eastern Pennsylvania a work of great beauty which for years has attracted half a million visitors annually. Henry F. du Pont has built at Winterthur, near Wilmington, a museum devoted to American household arts and decoration, an institution wholly unique which thousands visit each year. Neither Longwood nor Winterthur would exist if they had required public funds.

With government taking over more and more of the functions of private giving, our whole concept of benevolence toward one another changes radically. Already it may be noted in the attitude toward such of the eternal virtues as charity. Acceptance of a charitable gesture seems now to imply some loss of stature. This seems to me a very unfortunate point of view. Webster defines charity as "an act or feeling of affection or benevolence." In that sense, no matter how great our material well-being, each of us has been the recipient of charity from someone and, we would hope, would continue to be always.

We first receive charity from our parents who, as long as they live, give us their "affection and benevolence" as an act of love. We receive charity from our teachers who accept poorly paid positions in the feeling that imparting knowledge is an act of charity which fully compensates them for financial loss. In the same way, the clergy dispenses charity to all their congregations.

The exercise of charity, no matter how expressed, is beyond doubt a builder of character. It produces a spiritual uplift in the knowledge of a responsibility met and discharged to the best of one's ability. It is an important factor to Christian progress and, in that sense, increases the moral stature of both him who gives and him who receives.

What better example can either have to guide his own future conduct in this difficult world than the precept of a charitable act dictated by "affection or benevolence?" Is it not true that the affection and love given to us by our parents generates in us the will to do likewise with our own families? The beneficiary of a generous act has before him at all times the precept and example to conduct himself with the same generosity to others, for the act of charity in any form brings with it a realization of the obligation to do likewise within the limits of his ability. His own gesture of charity may not be in similar coin nor on a commensurate scale, but what he cannot reciprocate in kind, he may in kindness.

Once started, private charity, like a chain reaction, never ends. The good that is done by example and precept breeds in the recipient the same responsibility, desire, and obligation. It is like a wave of good will and comes finally to be a national rather than an individual attribute.

Our country has been charitable to an extent which is unheard of elsewhere in the world. What more generous national act could one conceive of than our various foreign-aid plans, however one may value their results? Where in any other land do we find private citizens devoting their resources so generously to the service of others less fortunate than themselves?

Our national characteristics are the summation of what we feel and do as individuals. And it seems to me that whatever spiritual stature we Americans have arises from the fact that, with us, charity in its highest sense has been regarded as an obligation and as an opportunity.

I do not like to contemplate what effect the decline of personal charity is likely to have on our national character. We see our government undertaking to do on our behalf those acts of charity that we used to be glad to do as individuals. We hear proposals that government guarantee security from the cradle to the grave; that government keep us in good health; that government educate us through grammar school, high school, and college. Certainly those are worthy objectives in themselves, but I do not see how that transfer of responsibility from individual to government can be accomplished without deterioration in our moral and spiritual fiber.

What of the recipient of government beneficence? Can he be expected to feel a sense of obligation to his fellows if what comes to him drips from the impersonal hands of government? We see already many examples of those who take handouts as though they were their due and whose only obligation, if any, is to vote right at the next election.

I am afraid that, in today's America, this is just one more of the traditional freedoms being worn away by a process of slow attrition. The immediate loss to us is perhaps bearable; the loss to future generations in my view is incalculable. The times of Stephen Girard and Matthew Vassar were indeed times of promise for this country's future greatness, with freedom of thought and action a real, tangible and cherished blessing.

To my mind, personal charity as a duty of citizenship was one of the great rewards which freedom brought to us. Perhaps it is not too late to bring it back as a source of great moral strength and satisfying spiritual growth.

THE OUTLOOK
FOR SCIENCE

Few subjects are so fascinating to magazine editors or to program chairmen than a detailed blueprint of the future. When they look my way, as happens occasionally, I flatly declare myself out. The shape of things to come seems to have been a preoccupation of man for centuries and, as a result, we have a record of innumerable prophecies, delivered in many cases with considerable authority and conviction. A review today reveals that the prophets were wrong far more often than they were right, and usually had erred on the side of pessimism with their forecasts falling far short of the actuality.

Wrong guesses in the field of science and technology have been numerous and the appraisals of hindsight make many appear ridiculous: The British economist who, in 1830, soberly noted that the labor of children down to the age of four would be necessary to sustain the world's growing population. Or the unfortunate American scientist—quite eminent, by the way—who a few months before Kitty Hawk proclaimed that the aeroplane was a scientific impossibility.

The instances in which prediction overlooked or underestimated scientific development, however, are even more striking: Jefferson, in arguing for the Louisiana Purchase, forecast that the entire area would be occupied *within two centuries*. Sir William Stanley Jevons gloomily estimated that the world's supply of coal would be exhausted by 1920. Or the enthusiast who foresaw the day when there would be "as many as a hundred" automobiles in every city!

The reason for this seeming ineptitude is simple. The future invariably takes its specific form from new principles which cannot be visualized by forecasters. In Jefferson's day, no one could have guessed at the revolution in transportation and its effect on human affairs. In 1850, no one could have foreseen the universal use of electricity and the uplift it gave to the public weal. In 1900, flight was something restricted to angels and birds. In 1925, the atom was a Pandora's box. And as late as 1950 who would have guessed that within a few years we would be seriously concerned over the *geopolitik* of outer space. In every age, there have been new principles just around the corner, and that corner is still ahead of us today. The future holds much of bright promise—of that we may be sure. The precise source of its brilliance is of little consequence.

We can face the future confidently, it seems to me, because, in the past twenty-five years or so, we have become increasingly conscious of the possibilities inherent in scientific research. The leverage which this activity has exerted upon the material progress of our times has been enormous despite the fact that only in comparatively recent years has it attained substantial and universal stature.

Science has quickened its tempo greatly since the days when I began as a worker in the laboratory. As an indication, the Du Pont Company in 1924 employed at its major research installation some 50 technical people. Today, there are more than 1,000 at that location alone, and the site, once shared with a golf course, a baseball diamond and a picnic grove, today resembles the campus of a fair-sized university.

When I first worked there at the Experimental Station, the facilities were relatively simple and the atmosphere decidedly informal. Proceedings were rather leisurely. I think it is now safe to confess that in those days, while keeping close watch on the instrument panel, I used to put my time on the graveyard shift to good advantage by practicing on my clarinet. I remember also during my lunch hour (or whatever a lunch hour on the graveyard shift is called) taking a swim on hot summer nights in the mill race which once supplied motive power for the powder mills.

A nocturnal eavesdropper would have gotten strange ideas about the nature of scientific inquiry on those premises.

Today, of course, American science has made enormous headway, and its most conspicuous achievement is the development of a corps of scientific personnel well trained and superbly competent. However one chooses to make the measurement— whether by manpower or by dollars—science has grown at a startling rate, particularly in America. Someone has pointed out that of all the scientists who ever lived, 95 per cent are still alive today, and in America the percentage would be even higher.

There is scarcely an industry today without full awareness of research and its promise. Twenty years ago, the chemical industry employed some 6,500 people in research work in its laboratories. There are approximately 35,000 today. The demand of all industry for competent research personnel has increased to the point where our colleges and universities are having grave difficulty in turning out qualified people in sufficient numbers.

The scientist in industry now enjoys a prestige which, considering the relatively short period of his ascendancy, is quite remarkable. In my early days, chemical engineers were a fairly uncommon breed. As a newly graduated zealot, I tried to explain to my friends just what I was and what I did. I regret to say that most of them, noting that I was principally concerned with pipes, valves, and stills, concluded that I must be a kind of glorified plumber, not nearly so interesting as the civil engineers with their high-laced boots or the man in the laboratory coat holding test-tube on high.

Research on the majestic scale evident today should give some assurance toward progress. While it is not a cash-and-carry activity, in which a given expenditure can guarantee a given result, it does provide us with the only valid basis we have for projecting future growth and development. The chemical industry, by way of example, has been research-minded from its beginnings and has had a rate of growth substantially greater than that of industry generally.

For our own Company, I can be somewhat more quantitative. We have reasonably good figures for research expenditures year by year since 1921. For the same period, we have a record of construction expenditures, and it seems to me the ratio of the two can fairly be taken as an index of cause and effect. The ratio of research dollars to construction dollars has averaged about one to three—for every dollar we have spent in our laboratories we have sooner or later spent $3 for new plants, products, and processes. This ratio, incidentally, has been reasonably constant over a period during which our annual research expenditures have increased from $1 million to something over $70 million. Or if one wishes to take an over-all look, we spent in the past twenty-five years approximately $600 million on research, excluding the cost of buildings and equipment, and, over the same period, approximately $1.8 billion for new plant and equipment. The ratio of one to three, valid both for the short and long term, can, I think, be extrapolated into the future with reasonable confidence.

I have no doubt that research will be as fruitful in the future as in the past. Startling new concepts are being formulated and, at any moment, one of them may emerge to transform the world as completely as those of Newton or Faraday or Einstein.

Actually, however, while limelight and applause are reserved for the spectacular developments, they represent only one side of the story. We all like, of course, to think about research in terms of the new product which springs from the test tube to the accompaniment of lyric headlines. At Du Pont, we like to talk about moistureproof cellophane, about neoprene, and about nylon. In addition to the prestige they have brought us, these developments have contributed largely to our corporate prosperity. In retrospect, however, I doubt that such individually spectacular accomplishments would account for as much as half of our growth over the last twenty-five to thirty years.

It is easy to overemphasize the new and, in doing so, to pay insufficient tribute to what might be called "bit-by-bit" research. By this, I mean the day-to-day effort which produces results which, over a short period, seem inconsequential, but which, over the long run, are extraordinarily important. It would be my guess that the average research man would have to work for two or three lifetimes before being associated with a development that hit the headlines.

He pays his way not by the spectacular, but by the creeping process of incremental accomplishment.

We enjoyed, for example, headlining the invention of the moistureproofing process which, for the first time, put cellophane on its commercial feet. That was quite an extraordinary development. On the other hand, during the last twenty-five years the output of a cellophane-casting machine has been increased something like sixfold, the output per man-hour fifteenfold, and the pounds produced per dollar of investment have been increased sevenfold. And it is these results which have made cellophane the important product it has become today, which have put its price at a sufficiently low level to make it generally useful. During any given year, process and product improvements, while solid and sure, are likely to be completely unspectacular. Over the long term, however, they make the difference between a static and a burgeoning economy, in that growth is enormously dependent upon the summation of small, sure improvements brought by unswerving devotion to research. This is the slow, steady way of progress.

Sometimes our research is directed toward a specific goal such as a new fiber, a new plastic, a new paint. More often it is not, and we plow our fields and sow our research seeds hoping that sufficiently important uses will turn up in other industries to make our effort worth while.

In spite of my distaste for prophecy, I can suggest a few important goals for research, particularly for chemical research. While I hasten to say I have no idea whether or not they will be reached by any given date, I am quite certain that one day they *will* be reached, be that day in this century or in the next:

Only the barest beginning has been made in the use of chemicals for the cure of disease. Today's antibiotics, the sulfa drugs, and anti-malarials, are surely only a hint of what the future will hold. Most illness must be related to body chemistry. What more natural solution than to use chemistry as the corrective agency?

Of greater importance is the maintenance of our body chemistry in good operating condition through proper nutrition. I do not mean here the 2,500 or more calories per day each of us requires as fuel, but of a surer and better understanding of the metabolism of the body and the specific chemical processes required to keep it healthy and vigorous. Our knowledge in this area is pathetically small, even though we have progressed far from the "tonic" area. How wonderful it would be if we could include in our diet the figurative ounce-of-prevention that would so well regulate our bodily processes as to make disease an historical curiosity.

There is also the problem of world food supply which may grow more pressing as the years advance and population increases. Here also chemistry has a role to play through new fertilizers, plant-growth regulants and hormones, pest-control agents, selective weed killers and veterinary chemicals.

There is a final goal, the attainment of which I fear is a long way off, its distance measured in decades rather than in years. How is mankind to supply his ever increasing requirements for energy? By this I mean energy in its broadest sense—not only the energy to drive our turbines, power plants, and automobiles, but the food energy required by the human body.

Over the years many have forecast the exhaustion of our sources of coal and oil. To be sure, they have all been overly pessimistic. It seems certain, however, that the day will come when exhaustion is indeed imminent. It is essential that we be ready with as good an alternative as possible.

Will atomic energy provide an answer? For a time, it was firmly believed that, in unleashing the energy of the atom, we had found the key to all future problems. As a member of the Manhattan Project group, I was present on that historic day under the silent stands of the Chicago University football stadium which saw the first sustained chain reaction ever produced by man. In the excitement of the occasion, I would have believed that atomic energy was the answer to anything.

Sober reflection, however, brings doubt. In due course, we will surely have central stations powered by the atom. But, as with coal and oil, there is a limit to the earth's supply of fissionable material, hence atomic energy, in spite of its importance, may be only an interim solution.

What we must devise eventually is some way of utilizing more fully the energy which comes to us from the sun. There is a *real* chain reaction—its source so placed as to defeat lethal radiations—generous in its output—and so long-lived that the day of its exhaustion lies in the inconceivably remote future. I sometimes wonder what our position would have been today had money and effort equivalent to that expended on atomic energy been devoted to the utilization of solar energy. Idle speculation —but the solution of the solar-energy problem cannot fail to be of more lasting benefit to mankind.

How the problem will be solved eventually I cannot guess. In the growing of crops, however, we have a technique for the utilization of solar energy which is deficient only in degree. Today, the best thermal efficiency we can obtain in agriculture is a few tenths of 1 per cent of the energy the sun lavishes on our land. If this could be increased by a factor of ten, the problem of energy and food would be solved for many hundreds of years to come.

The solution would appear to depend on some way of hastening, through better utilization of solar energy, the "fixation," if you will, of the carbon dioxide in the atmosphere as burnable, eatable, usable fuel. I say usable advisedly because the chemical industry has a long-term problem too, and that is to supply itself with adequate quantities of organic carbon from which to synthesize not only its present extensive list of products, but those it will develop in the future. We now depend largely upon petroleum and coal, and to a lesser extent on agricultural by-products. Combustible fuel, organic raw material, and food are all facets of the over-all problem of future energy supply, and no solution is adequate which does not deal with all.

Here, then, is chemistry's most challenging goal —to devise a biological solar storage battery which, through acceleration of the processes of plant biology, will provide not only energy, but food and raw materials as well. I am sure that goal will be reached on some fine and glorious day and, in reaching it, chemistry will have accomplished its greatest feat.

From all this, it may be gathered that I expect the future to be bright, that there are still goals worth striving for, and that, in reaching them, chemistry as a science and as an industry will play an important part. None of this, however, can happen automatically, and there are qualifications—two of them, in fact—of substantial and controlling import for future progress.

The first qualification is simple and straightforward. It is that this nation must have a balanced research program, which means that it must supplement its applied research with an amount of fundamental research sufficient to provide the basic information upon which all scientific progress depends. We define fundamental research as inquiry into the fundamentals of nature without specific commercial objective. A substantial amount of such research is now being done by industry. The major responsibility, however, must rest with our universities, for only they can provide the atmosphere in which truly fundamental scientific inquiry can properly flourish. The problem is not so much one of persuasion as of finance; it is here that industry, by supporting academic fundamental science, can at the same time serve its stockholders and supply a public need.

The second qualification which must be attached to technological progress is more subtle, and more difficult to express. It is simply that an atmosphere be provided which will persuade men to exercise in highest degree the talents they possess.

I doubt that there has been any time throughout recorded history when advances in man's material well-being have been made so rapidly and so consistently as in our country during the past two hundred years. Americans have been accused of being gross materialists, of thinking more of things and possessions than of ideas and ideals. To me, these accusations have always seemed to have the flavor of sour grapes. I doubt very much that there is any inherent difference between Americans and citizens of other countries in terms of their material desires. The difference seems to me simply one of the extent to which those goals have been attained.

Our progress cannot be ascribed, except in part, to natural resources or benign circumstance. What we have had has been freedom, and, through freedom, the incentive to aspire to any heights we felt we could reach; to reap and to hold the rewards of our accomplishment. We have witnessed over nearly two centuries the inherent virtue of the carrot over the stick.

But in looking toward the future, we should realize that, in recent years through our system of extreme progressive taxation, we have seriously impaired the incentive of financial reward. I hold no brief for money *per se*. It is a nice thing to have, in quantities large or small, not because one sits and admires it, like Midas, but because, as I have elaborated in a previous chapter, of the constructive things it enables one to do.

With scientific effort becoming to an increasing degree the prodigy of industry and exposed as such to the same penalties its parent body must bear, the health of our industrial institutions is clearly a factor in the advancement of science.

There are various ways in which industry can be handicapped and hamstrung by an unwise government. Most of them have at one time or another been applied, somewhere, usually with the result that the industry or the government—or occasionally both—have collapsed under the strain.

Of all such strictures, deliberate or inadvertent,

none has been potentially so disastrous as that which renders accomplishment unattractive and the will to achieve a reproach.

Industry has traditionally, and by its very nature, depended primarily upon financial reward for accomplishment. If we agree that a prerequisite of a successful business is sound and able management, then loss of the incentives which have proved attractive must inevitably diminish the chances of satisfactory progress. For unless business can offer the hope of financial reward, I do not see an alternative which will tempt in sufficient numbers the men and women who will fill our upper management ranks a generation or so in the future. The problem arises not so much for mature people; it has its beginnings in earliest manhood. For we must persuade young people, first to put enough effort and thought into their jobs to develop and display their potential, second to accept more responsible positions when offered, and finally to embrace the devotion and single-mindedness which are necessary to make positions of top responsibility effective.

The important thing for the nation's future is to ensure insofar as possible that every one of our people, in science and elsewhere, do the utmost of which he is capable. To that end, we should have available every incentive ingenious minds can devise. And it seems to me a great catastrophe when financial incentive, traditionally one of the most persuasive, is allowed to fall by the wayside.

To be sure, financial reward is only one mark of accomplishment. Thus far, however, it is the only one which has been subjected to the arthritis of "progressive" taxation. I can only hope that the tax collector of the future will not discover ways to levy upon the less divisible inducements and satisfactions of life.

How distressing it would be, for example, if the Misses Kim Novak, Brigitte Bardot, and similarly spectacular females be required to wear veils or other concealing garments in order that their competitive edge over less fortunate sisters be equalized. Or that Messrs. Heifetz and Menuhin be required to play slightly off key lest they put to shame less able contemporaries. Or had Ernest Lawrence been asked to share, in some way yet to be devised, 91 per cent of the prestige associated with his Nobel Prize.

If these possibilities appear preposterous, let us only reflect that they are nothing more than the extension of current tax philosophies into non-financial areas. And, if we can regard money as only one of the rewards of man, we can see, I think, the inequity of singling it out for special treatment.

I have no particular suggestion as to how the law should be revised. My only contention is that, in levying any tax, we should place it in such a way as to be the least possible burden on the growth of the economy. And, in my opinion, the steep ascent of personal taxation slows down the advance of the economy to a degree far overbalancing the revenue collected in the process.

The development of our economy will depend, in the future as in the past, on individual personal achievement. Any incentive which furthers this end is good business—and good government. Prestige, public approbation, spiritual satisfaction, financial reward—we need them all, not only because we are concerned about the individual recipient, but because a nation's progress is in direct proportion to its people's willingness to strive and struggle for whatever goal seems worth while. If we are successful in recapturing that atmosphere of freedom, incentive, and self-respect, the future will be boundless indeed.